THE GOOGLE BOYS

THE GOOGLE BOYS

Sergey Brin and Larry Page
In Their Own Words

EDITED BY GEORGE BEAHM

AN AGATE IMPRINT

CHICAGO

Library of Congress Cataloging-in-Publication Data

The Google boys : Sergey Brin and Larry Page in their own words / edited by George Beahm.
    pages cm -- (In their own words)
Summary: ""A collection of direct quotes from Larry Page and Sergey Brin, the founders of Google, on topics related to business, entrepreneurship, and life"--Provided by publisher"-- Provided by publisher.
 Includes bibliographical references and index.
 ISBN-13: 978-1-932841-88-6 (paperback)
 ISBN-10: 1-932841-88-1 (paperback)
1. Google (Firm) 2. Brin, Sergey, 1973---Quotations. 3. Page, Larry, 1973---Quotations. 4. Businesspeople--United States--Quotations. I. Brin, Sergey, 1973- II. Page, Larry, 1973- III. Beahm, George.
 HD9696.8.U64G66525 2014
 338.7'6102504--dc23

                         2014017694

10 9 8 7 6 5 4 3 2 1

B2 is an imprint of Agate Publishing. Agate books are available in bulk at discount prices. For more information, go to agatepublishing.com

To Sarah, David, and Jessica

TABLE OF CONTENTS

INTRODUCTION

Google Organizing the World's Knowledge

The greatest crisis facing us is...in the organization and accessibility of human knowledge. We own an enormous "encyclopedia," which isn't even arranged alphabetically. Our "file cards" are spilled on the floor, nor were they ever in order. The answers we want may be buried somewhere in the heap, but it might take a lifetime to locate two already known facts, place them side by side, and derive a third fact, the one we urgently need.

Call it the crisis of the librarian.

We need a new "specialist" who is not a specialist, but a synthesist. We need a new science to be the perfect secretary to all other sciences.

But we are not likely to get either one in a hurry and we have a powerful lot of grief before us in the meantime.

—ROBERT A. HEINLEIN IN 1950

Ten years ago, a company with the odd name of "Google" went public, selling shares for $85 each. Back then, no one could figure out how to monetize search. Existing ad models, fashioned after print ads, were ineffective. But by placing classified ads on a Google search page with subject matter related to the search itself—by creating targeted ads, in other words—Google created a brand-new ad model that proved very effective: a click-through on an ad meant a commission paid from the vendor directly to the company.

As of May 2014, after its stock split, Google shares now sell for $536, and the company's prime mover is its online search engine, which generates 13.1 billion searches a month, according to comScore, Inc. Google's total ad revenue, drawn predominantly from targeted AdWords, brought the company $55.5 billion in sales in 2013. The Google search engine, noted comScore, had a 67.5 percent search share in March 2014.

Well poised for the future, Google has more than enough money in its coffers to invest long term in speculative projects, which its co-founder Larry Page calls "moon shots." Some of these projects include Google Glass (a wearable computer in the form of eyeglasses, for $1,500), self-driving cars, and Calico, a health initiative to research the extension of human life.

Google co-founders Larry Page and Sergey Brin even announced an ambitious project called Virgle, with a goal of establishing a colony on Mars. People were asked to submit 30-second videos on why they should be picked for this mission. Google created detailed Web pages filled with information about every aspect of Virgle, from its selection process to the specifics of the Mars colony itself, and at least one author writing about Google was fooled—it was not a legitimate Google project but an elaborate hoax.

Page and Brin delight in such pranks, which are timed for release on the first of April every year. They recall another prominent computer figure who also loved to play pranks: Steve "Woz" Wozniak, a co-founder of Apple. (Woz once developed a small electronic device that interfered with television reception; the unsuspecting victims, attempting to clear up the picture, would fiddle with the "rabbit ears" on top of the television set and even contort their bodies into pretzel-like shapes to improve reception.)

But apart from its founders' appreciation of whimsy, the ubiquity of its search engine, and its billions of dollars in ad revenue, Google did not begin with a hunger for fame or financial success. Unlike the other dot-coms of its time, which often followed a predictable model—create a product, get investor funding, and hope to retire young and rich—Google began with a hunger for information. When they started out, Page and Brin were just two Stanford graduate students searching for algorithms that would yield better results for a search engine they dubbed BackRub, which would later develop into Google.

BackRub is 18 years in the past, and Page and Brin are now highly respected, established figures in the tech industry. They no longer spend hours hunched over keyboards writing code; they've got talented, smart employees who can do that. What they do is run a multi-billion-dollar company that's the tech elephant in the room, and has a long-range vision to match.

Moreover, Page and Brin—unlike industry icons like Steve Jobs or Bill Gates—have spent as little time as possible in front of the media. It's not that they are camera shy; they simply see public relations and marketing as support functions, and thus of secondary concern. In fact, in the early years, Page told the PR department that he'd allot only eight hours annually for interviews, press appearances, and press releases. As a result, when Larry Page and Sergey Brin spare time to speak, people listen carefully.

This book brings together hand-selected quotes from interviews, online postings, the annual

Google founders' letter, personal blogs, public appearances, and select press releases. What emerges is a portrait in words of both men, who have created a business model in Google that may well be a template for businesses in the future.

Businesspeople at all levels will find these quotations intriguing, thought-provoking, challenging, and visionary. Page and Brin's ideas can be used as tools to rethink your business, spark new ideas, and open unexplored avenues for further thought.

And if you need more information, you can always Google it.

Actually, more and more librarians love Google. They use it. They do an excellent job helping people find answers on the Internet in addition to using their book collections. Finding information still requires skill. It's just that you can go much further now. Google is a tool for librarians just as it's a tool for anyone who wants to use it.

—SERGEY BRIN, *PLAYBOY*, SEPTEMBER 2004

QUOTATIONS

Early Years

....

Family's First Computer

Larry Page: [M]y dad was a computer science professor, so we had computers really early. The first computer we owned as a family was in 1978, the Exidy Sorcerer. It was popular in Europe but never in the US. It had 32K memory. My brother had to write the operating system.

—*San Francisco Chronicle*, December 31, 2000

....

Stanford University

Page: I had decided I was either going to be a professor or start a company. I was really excited to get into Stanford. There wasn't any better place to go for that kind of aspiration. I always wanted to go to Silicon Valley.

—*The Search: How Google and Its Rivals Rewrote the Rules of Business and Transformed Our Culture*, 2005

Academia

Page: There are things I want to work on that are very speculative, and Stanford is a great place to do things like that. ...If you're doing something you're not sure is going to work at all, a company probably isn't the right place to be doing it.

—Interview for Academy of Achievement,
October 28, 2000

Serendipity

Page: We didn't start out to do a search engine at all. In late 1995, I started collecting the links on the Web because my [faculty] advisor and I decided that would be a good thing to do. We didn't know exactly what I was gonna do with it. But it seemed like no one was really looking at the links on the Web—you know, which pages link to which pages. ...I figured I could get a dissertation and do something fun and perhaps practical at the same time, which is really what motivates me.

—"Corporate Valley Presents: Exclusive Interview of
Larry Page and Sergey Brin," January 24, 2013

● ●

Following Dreams

Page: I have a story about following dreams…it's a story about finding a path to make those dreams real.…

Well, I had one of those dreams when I was 23. When I suddenly woke up, I was thinking: What if we could download the whole Web, and just keep the links, and…I grabbed a pen and started writing!…Amazingly, I had no thought of building a search engine. The idea wasn't even on the radar. But much later, we happened upon a better way of ranking Web pages to make a really great search engine, and Google was born. When a really great dream shows up, grab it!

—University of Michigan commencement speech,
May 2, 2009

· ·

Business Opportunity

Page: I think part of the reason we're successful so far is that originally, we didn't really want to start a business. We were doing research at Stanford University. Google sort of came out of that. And we didn't even intend to build a search engine originally. We were just interested in the Web and interested in data mining. And then we ended up with search technology that we realized was really good. And we built the search engine. Then we told our friends about it and our professors. Pretty soon, about 10,000 people a day were using it.

We realized by talking to all the CEOs of search companies—which were really turning into portals—that commercially, no one was going to develop search engines. They said, "Oh, we don't really care about our search engine." And we realized there was a huge business opportunity and that nobody else was going to work on it.

—*Bloomberg Businessweek*, May 2, 2004

Initial Funding

Sergey Brin: [Andy Bechtolsheim] gave us a check for $100,000. The check was made out to "Google Inc.," which didn't exist at the time—which was a big problem. So we had to quickly get a lawyer, and we set up the company. ...The check sat in my desktop drawer for a month. I was afraid I'd lose it. But until it really happened, until then, it had sort of been this intermediate state. ...But when he wrote the check—well, it certainly does speed things up.

—"The Lost Google Tapes," January 2000

Celebrating Funding

Brin and Page breakfasted at Burger King after receiving Bechtolsheim's initial funding:

Page: We thought we should [eat] something that tasted really good, though it was really unhealthy. And it was cheap. It seemed like the right combination of ways to celebrate the funding.

—*The Search*, 2005

••

Work Hours

In 1999, Google still operated out of a garage in a suburban house at 232 Santa Margarita Avenue in Menlo Park, California. Google then had six full-time employees. Brin said of his and Page's work hours at the time:

Brin: We're working much, much harder than we would in a normal job. It's not a 40-hour-a-week job.

We've been trying to cut down. When we started, we'd be working upwards of 12 hours a day, 6 days a week. But we have been trying to cut down, because we think this isn't necessarily most productive. We try hard to take at least one of the weekend days off, and at times both or at least portions of both.

Anyway, we're trying to push it down below 60 hours.

—*Stern* magazine, January 1999

· ·

Growth of Google

Brin: One thing is that we have ten or twenty thousand people to help us. Certainly I am not pulling all-nighters all the time like we were in the garage, when we were only three to four people doing everything. So now I have vastly more help, and, I think, concern about using our time efficiently, having good judgment, making good decisions.

—*Reuters*, May 9, 2008

Products and Technology

••

Scope of Google

Page: If you printed out the index, it would be 70 miles high now. We have all this computation. We have about 6,000 computers. So we have a lot of resources available. We have enough space to store like 100 copies of the whole Web. So you have a really interesting sort of confluence of a lot of different things: a lot of computation, a lot of data that didn't used to be available.

—Interview for Academy of Achievement,
October 28, 2000

••

Better Search Engine

Page: We settled on looking at the link structure on the Web—how to grab all the links and analyze them and do something interesting. We eventually wound up with a way to rank Web pages based on the link, then realized we could build a better search engine. And we did just that.

—*Michigan Engineer*, Spring/Summer 2001

....

Artificial Intelligence

Page: One of my favorite things is artificial intelligence, but it has gotten a very bad rap...but my prediction is that when AI happens, it's going to be a lot of computation and not so much clever algorithms....My theory is that if you look at your programming, your DNA, it's about 600 megabytes compressed, so it's smaller than any modern operating system, smaller than Linux or Windows or anything like that. Your whole operating system—that includes booting up your brain, by definition. So your program algorithms probably aren't that complicated, it's probably more about the overall computation, but that's my guess.

We have some people at Google who are really trying to build artificial intelligence and to do it on a large scale.... To do the perfect job of search, you could ask any query and it would give you the perfect answer and that would be artificial intelligence, based on everything being on the Web, which is a pretty close approximation. We're lucky enough to be working incrementally closer to that, but again, very, very few people are working on this, and I don't think it's as far off as people think.

—Address at the American Association for the
Advancement of Science, February 2007

• •

Ideal Searcher

Brin: The ideal searcher would be something with human intelligence and all [the] knowledge in the world. Currently, humans have the former and computers have the latter (well, close to it), so you do have to sift through search results. In the future, who knows...

—*.com–LIVE*, November 4, 1999

• •

Perfect Search Engine

Brin: It would be the mind of God.

—*Red Herring*, July 16, 2002

• •

Design

Page: Our goal is to design everything so it's beautifully simple.

—Google's July 2013 Q2 earnings call

••

Google as Reference Librarian

Page: The Web is more of a superlibrarian. Imagine if you had a reference librarian who had all the knowledge of Google but could also answer instantly with all that knowledge. That would really change the world.

—*Bloomberg Businessweek*, May 2, 2004

••

Books Online

Brin: Call me weird, but I think there are a lot of advantages to reading books online. You don't have to look at it at a funny angle, and today's monitors have better resolution than ever.

—*USA Today*, October 28, 2008

••

Google Books

On Google's 2008 agreement with the Authors Guild and the Association of American Publishers to expand online access to in-copyright books and materials through Google Books:

Brin: While this agreement is a real win-win for all of us, the real victors are all the readers. The tremendous wealth of knowledge that lies within the books of the world will now be at their fingertips.

—Google press release, October 28, 2008

••

Google Glass

Brin: My vision when we started Google 15 years ago was that eventually you wouldn't have to have a search query at all—you would just have information come to you as you needed it. This is, now, 15 years later, sort of the first form factor that I think can deliver that vision when you're out and about and on the street, talking to people and so forth.

—*TED Talks*, February 2013

● ●

"I'm Feeling Lucky" Option for Google's Search Engine

Brin: The reason it's called "I'm Feeling Lucky" is of course [that it's] a pretty damn ambitious goal. I mean, to get the exact right one thing without even giving you a list of choices—and so you have to feel a little bit lucky if you're gonna try that with one go.

—*Marketplace*, November 19, 2007

● ●

"Jew Watch" Website

After an anti-Semitic website appeared in a prominent position in Google search results for the word "Jew":

Brin: I certainly am very offended by the site, but the objectivity of our rankings is one of our very important principles.

—*Moment*, February–March 2007

••

Products

After affirming the importance of improving existing products:

Page: But periodically, every *n* years, you should work on something new that you think is really amazing. The trick is coming up with those products. I could probably give you a list of 10 major things that are wrong with email. I try to maintain lists like that in my head.

—*Wired*, January 17, 2013

••

Self-Driving Cars

Page: We've had a team working on [self-driving cars] and we've driven over 200,000 miles now with no incidents. And it's really amazing to ride in one of these cars. It's just almost a life-changing experience. You sit down, you drive through a parking lot, and you're like, "Why am I driving?"

—"Beyond Today," speech at Zeitgeist 2012

···

Smartphones

Page: I think, you know, it's really exciting to see that everyone in the world is gonna get a smartphone now. And for many people, for most people, probably, in the world, it's gonna be their first computer. It's not a question of "if" now, it's just a question of when.

—"Beyond Today," speech at Zeitgeist 2012

···

Think Crazy

Page: Currently, probably, we're doing something that all of you think is crazy—we're making self-driving cars. But, you know, I have young kids. I imagine many of you do. Imagine, you know, 10 or 12 years from now, they're turning 16. How happy will you be to have them being taught [to drive] by a car? They can still drive; they think they're driving. They just can't kill themselves or anyone else. They'll still have the illusion of driving if you like. Wouldn't that be a better world? And that's the leading cause of death for 16-year-olds, right, is car crashes in the US. So you just think about those kind[s] of things, and it's easy to think they're crazy now.

—Q & A at Zeitgeist Americas 2012

Think Long Term

Page: We have always tried to concentrate on the long term, and to place bets on technology we believe will have a significant impact over time. It's hard to imagine now, but when we started Google, most people thought search was a solved problem and that there was no money to be made apart from some banner advertising. We felt the exact opposite: that search quality was very poor, and that awesome user experiences would clearly make money.

—Google's "2012 Update from the CEO"

Moon Shots

Page: I'm not proposing that we spend all of our money on those kinds of speculative things. But we should be spending a commensurate amount with what normal types of companies spend on research and development and spend it on things that are a little more long term and a little more ambitious than people normally would. More like moon shots.

—*Time,* September 30, 2013

••

Toothbrush Test

The means by which Google determines what they will work on:

Page: Do you use it as often as you use your toothbrush?

—"Beyond Today," speech at Zeitgeist 2012

••

Mission of Google

Brin: [O]ur mission is to make the world's information accessible and useful. And that means all of the world's information, which now, in our index, numbers over a billion documents, and it's an incredible resource. In history, you have never had access to just pretty much all of the world's information in seconds, and we have that now, and to make it really useful, you have to have a way of finding whatever it is that you want. That's precisely what we work on at Google. My hope is to provide instant access to any information anybody ever wants in the future.

—Interview for Academy of Achievement, October 28, 2000

Innovation and Competition

. . . .

Competitors

Page: For a lot of companies, it's useful for them to feel like they have an obvious competitor and to rally around that. I personally believe that it's better to shoot higher. You don't want to be looking at your competitors. You want to be looking at what's possible and how to make the world better.

—*Bloomberg Businessweek*, April 4, 2012

. . . .

Big Bets

Page: How exciting is it to come to work if the best you can do is trounce some other company that does roughly the same thing? That's why most companies decay slowly over time. They tend to do approximately what they did before, with a few minor changes. It's natural for people to want to work on things that they know aren't going to fail. But incremental improvement is guaranteed to be obsolete over time. Especially in technology, where you know there's going to be non-incremental change.

—*Wired*, January 17, 2013

Multiple Goals

Page: For me, it was always unsatisfying if you look at companies that get very big and they're just doing one thing. Ideally, if you have more people and more resources, you can get more things solved. We've kind of always had that philosophy.

—*Time,* September 30, 2013

70/20/10

Page: There's a reason we talk about 70/20/10, where 70 percent of our resources are spent in our core business and 10 percent end up in unrelated projects, like energy or whatever. [The other 20 percent goes to projects adjacent to the core business.] Actually, it's a struggle to get it to even be 10 percent. People might think we're wasting money or whatever. But that's where all our new stuff has come from.

—*Fortune,* May 1, 2008

··

"Great just isn't good enough."

From the Google company website:

We see being great at something as a starting point, not an endpoint. We set ourselves goals we know we can't reach yet, because we know that by stretching to meet them, we can get further than we expected. Through innovation and iteration, we aim to take things that work well and improve upon them in unexpected ways.

— "Ten Things We Know to Be True,"
Google company website

··

Fast Decision-Making

Page: One of the interesting things we noticed was that companies correlate on decision-making and speed of decision-making. There are basically no companies that have good slow decisions. There are only companies that have good fast decisions. So I think that's also a natural thing: As companies get bigger, they tend to slow down decision-making. And that's pretty tragic.

—Q & A with Eric Schmidt at
Zeitgeist Americas 2011

●●

Dot-com Zeitgeist

Page: We knew a lot of things people were doing weren't sustainable, and that made it hard for us to operate. We couldn't get good people for reasonable prices. We couldn't get office space. It was a hypercompetitive time. We had the opportunity to invest in 100 or more companies and didn't invest in any of them. I guess we lost a lot of money in the short term—but not in the long term.

—*Playboy*, September 2004

●●

Patent Infringements

Page: Obviously, we held a lot of search patents, for example. We have somehow been successful without suing other people over intellectual property.

So for us, the general trend of the industry toward being a lot more litigious somehow has just been—it has been a sad thing. There is a lot of money going to lawyers and things, instead of building great products for users. I think that companies usually get into that when they're toward the end of their life cycle or they don't have confidence in their abilities to compete naturally.

—*Bloomberg Businessweek*, April 4, 2012

Closed Systems

Page: Virtually everything that we want to do, I think, is somewhat at odds with, you know, locking down all of your information for uses that you haven't contemplated yet. So, you know, that's something I worry about. I think it's a very important thing.

We don't actually know how the Internet's gonna work 10 years from now. So it's kind of, I think, a mistake to start carving out large classes of things that you don't really understand yet, that you don't want to let people do. I think that's kind of the approach that a lot of regulators are taking, which I think is sad.

—Q & A at Zeitgeist Americas 2012

••

Open vs. Closed Systems

Page: Our philosophy has always been to get our products out to as many people as possible. Unfortunately, that's not always easy in this day and age. The Web has been great; we were able to get products out to everyone, quickly and with high quality. Now we're going backward with a lot of platforms that are out there. Companies are trying to wall everything off, and I think that impedes the rate of innovation.

—*Wired*, January 17, 2013

Open-Source OS Driving Innovation

Page: I remember first meeting Andy Rubin, the creator of Android, back in 2004. At the time, developing apps for mobile devices was incredibly painful. We had a closet full of over 100 phones, and we were building our software pretty much one device at a time. Andy believed that aligning standards around an open-source operating system would drive innovation across the mobile industry. At the time, most people thought he was nuts.

Fast forward to today. Android is on fire, and the pace of mobile innovation has never been greater. Over 850,000 devices are activated daily through a network of 55 manufacturers and more than 300 carriers. Android is a tremendous example of the power of partnership, and it just gets better with each version. The latest update, Ice Cream Sandwich, has a beautiful interface that adapts to the form of the device. Whether it's on a phone or tablet, the software works seamlessly.

—Google's "2012 Update from the CEO"

● ●

Facebook's Major Fail

Brin: You have to play by their rules, which are really restrictive. The kind of environment that we developed Google in, the reason that we were able to develop a search engine, is [that] the Web was so open. Once you get too many rules, that will stifle innovation.

—*Time*, April 16, 2012

● ●

Facebook's Closed Data

Page: I think it's been unfortunate that Facebook has been pretty closed with their data....We don't generally turn it down when it's offered to us.

...So we said, "We'll only participate with people who have reciprocity." And we're still waiting.

I think the idea that, you know, you'd hold your users hostage, kind of, and the absence of reasons for it....You know, they'd hold their users' data.

—*Charlie Rose*, May 21, 2012

. . . .

Microsoft Contemplates Buying Yahoo

Brin: The Internet has evolved from open standards, having a diversity of companies, and when you start to have companies that control the operating system, control the browsers, they really tie up the top websites, and can be used to manipulate stuff in various ways. I think that's unnerving.

—Associated Press, February 21, 2008

. . . .

Microsoft's Search-and-Destroy Strategy

Brin: I worry about Microsoft. I don't worry about competing with them, but they've stated that they really want to destroy Google. I feel like they've left a lot of companies by the wayside.

—*Time*, February 20, 2006

· ·

Opportunities Untapped

Page: You may say that Apple only does a very, very small number of things, and that's working pretty well for them. But I find that unsatisfying. I feel like there are all these opportunities in the world to use technology to make people's lives better. At Google we're attacking maybe 0.1 percent of that space. And all the tech companies combined are only at like 1 percent. That means there's 99 percent virgin territory.

—*Wired*, January 17, 2013

· ·

Staying Focused

Brin: Basically, we want to stay focused on what we do well, which is getting people to more useful information. We don't want to be building out lots of services, which is what other companies do well, like Yahoo.

—"The Lost Google Tapes," January 2000

. . . .

Web Portals

Page: Most portals show their own content above content elsewhere on the Web. We feel that's a conflict of interest, analogous to taking money for search results. Their search engine doesn't necessarily provide the best results; it provides the portal's results. Google conscientiously tries to stay away from that. We want to get you out of Google and to the right place as fast as possible. It's a very different model.

—*Playboy*, September 2004

. . . .

Forward Thinking

Page: Companies tend to get comfortable doing what they've always done, with a few minor tweaks. It's only natural to want to work on the things you know. But incremental improvement is guaranteed to be obsolete over time.

—Google's April 2013 Q1 earnings call

●●●

Leverage

Page: [Google's computers can] aggregate content; we can process it, rank it; we can do lots of things that are valuable. We can build systems that let lots of people create content themselves. That's really where our leverage is.

—*Googled,* 2009

●●●

Mobile

Page: Computing is moving onto mobile. Even if I have a computer next to me, I'll still be on my mobile device.

—*New York Times,* August 15, 2011

• •

Mobile Devices Monetized

In the wake of a prematurely released, disappointing quarterly earnings report, which caused investors to fear that mobile search would be less profitable than PC-based search:

Page: There's so much opportunity based on always having a computer with you, knowing where it is and so on. I think, you know, monetization is gonna go up. Opportunities are gonna go up, products are gonna work better for people....There will be some disruption as people go through those changes. But a lot of the things we do work great on a smartphone.

—Q & A at Zeitgeist Americas 2012

Business Principles

∙∙∙

Commercialization

Page: [Xerox] PARC had a tremendous research organization, and they invented many of the tools of modern computing. But they weren't focused on commercialization. You need both....I realized that there's a lot of sad stories about inventors like Nikola Tesla, amazing people who didn't have much impact, because they never turned their inventions into businesses.

—*Wired*, January 17, 2013

∙∙∙

Product Line Focus

Page: Last April, I began by reorganizing the management team around our core products to improve responsibility and accountability across Google. I also kicked off a big cleanup. Google has so many opportunities that, unless we make some hard choices, we end up spreading ourselves too thin and don't have the impact we want. So we have closed or combined over 30 products.

—Google's "2012 Update from the CEO"

Dual Voting Class Stock Structure

Page and Brin: We believe a dual class voting structure will enable Google, as a public company, to retain many of the positive aspects of being private. We understand some investors do not favor dual class structures. Some may believe that our dual class structure will give us the ability to take actions that benefit us, but not Google's shareholders as a whole. We have considered this point of view carefully, and we and the board have not made our decision lightly. We are convinced that everyone associated with Google—including new investors—will benefit from this structure. However, you should be aware that Google and its shareholders may not realize these intended benefits.

—"Letter from the Founders" in Amendment 9 to Form S-1, August 18, 2004

· ·

"It's best to do one thing really, really well."

From the Google company website:
We do search….Through continued iteration on
difficult problems, we've been able to solve com-
plex issues and provide continuous improvements
to a service that already makes finding information a fast and seamless experience for millions
of people.

— "Ten Things We Know to Be True,"
Google company website

· ·

Hiring Smart People

Page: We don't really know that the way we hire
at Google is optimal, and we're trying to improve
it all the time. We obviously hire a lot of smart
people. We also hire people who have different
kinds of skills, and we hire people who work on
computers, and do construction, and many, many
other things.

—*Fortune*, January 31, 2008

••

Hiring Passionate People

Brin: This is where you want to make sure you are hiring employees because they love to work here, they love to create things, and they're not here primarily for the money. Although when they do create something valuable you want to reward them. That's when these things really pay off. I like to think we're putting a lot of investment in things that matter a lot more when you're not having such a great time as a company. I'm sure things will fluctuate.

—*Fortune*, January 31, 2008

••

Money

Page's turn-down response, when company engineers told him that they could add $80 million in annual revenue if they added sponsored links to image-search results:

Page: We're not making enough money already?

—*Time*, February 20, 2006

···

Strategy

Page: We don't generally talk about our strategy
… because it's strategic. I would rather have people think we're confused than let our competitors
know what we're going to do.

—Time, February 20, 2006

···

Auction-based IPO

Page and Brin: Many companies going public
have suffered from unreasonable speculation,
small initial share float, and stock price volatility
that hurt them and their investors in the long run.
We believe that our auction-based IPO will mini-
mize these problems, though there is no guaran-
tee that it will.

—"Letter from the Founders" in Amendment 9 to
Form S-1, August 18, 2004

Trust in Results

Page: Whenever you do a search, you're trusting us to give you the right things. We take that very seriously. We have a pretty good reputation in that regard. I think people see us as willing to take positions that some might find weird initially. But we definitely can explain why we did it, and we're up front about that.

—*Fortune*, January 31, 2008

Media and Advertising

•••

Media

Page: So I think that's one important thing to focus on, is trying to get people to think things are possible, and the way you do that is you start with the media. That's really where most people are paying attention. I was just going to use the example of [television show] *CSI: Crime Scene Investigation*....I think probably we'll have more crime scene investigators than we'll ever need because of that show. It wouldn't surprise me. It's amazing the things that the media can really have an impact on.

—Address at the American Association for the Advancement of Science, February 2007

••

Advertising (in 1999)

In 1999, when Google still operated out of a garage:

Brin: Right now, we're thinking about generating some revenue. We have a number of ways [of] doing that. One thing is we can put up some advertising. The key there is to put up advertising that will be really useful to our users and not slow down our site. That way, we won't push people away from our site, but we'll still take in some revenue. Another way would be co-branding. Provide the backend search engine to other sites.

—*Stern* magazine, January 1999

••

Advertising Campaigns

Brin: We've resisted the temptation, at least thus far, to have, you know, these big advertising campaigns....I mean, I'm not sure it's the right thing to do....I am concerned about long-term profitability.

—"The Lost Google Tapes," January 2000

AdWords

Brin: Our goal is to create a single and complete advertising system. Diversity in our advertising and publisher base continues to be central to our business and is important to our long-term success. Advertisers large and small use Google to reach their target audiences easily and get measurable ROI.... As more and more users look for local information online, we must continue to improve our ability to attract local advertisers. This year we partnered with companies...to help us bring more business information online and convert more small businesses into happy Google customers. Small business is big business.

—Google Annual Report, 2006

••

Ethics of Advertising

Brin: Somebody's always upset no matter what we do. We have to make a decision; otherwise there's a never-ending debate. Some issues are crystal clear. When they're less clear and opinions differ, sometimes we have to break a tie. For example, we don't accept ads for hard liquor, but we accept ads for wine. It's just a personal preference. We don't allow gun ads, and the gun lobby got upset about that. We don't try to put our sense of ethics into the search results, but we do when it comes to advertising.

—Playboy, September 2004

••

Paid Inclusion Ads

Brin: We make it clear when something is paid for. Our advertising is off to the side and in a couple of slots across the top. Ads are clearly marked. There's a clear, large wall between the objective search results and the ads, which have commercial influence. ... At Google, the search results cannot be bought or paid for.

—Playboy, September 2004

Winning

When an employee, Douglas Edwards, suggested that, "In a world where all search engines are equal, we'll need to rely on branding to differentiate us from everyone else":

Page: If we can't win on quality, we shouldn't win at all.

—I'm Feeling Lucky, 2011

•••

"You can make money without doing evil."

From the Google company website:

Google is a business. The revenue we generate is derived from offering search technology to companies and from the sale of advertising displayed on our site and on other sites across the Web. Hundreds of thousands of advertisers worldwide use AdWords to promote their products; hundreds of thousands of publishers take advantage of our AdSense program to deliver ads relevant to their site content. To ensure that we're ultimately serving all our users (whether they are advertisers or not), we have a set of guiding principles for our advertising programs and practices: We don't allow ads to be displayed on our results pages unless they are relevant where they are shown.... We don't accept pop-up advertising....We never manipulate rankings to put our partners higher in our search results, and no one can buy better PageRank.

—"Ten Things We Know to Be True,"
Google company website

User Experience

. . . .

Tardiness

When asked, in 1999, regarding search engines, "Aren't you rather late to the game?":

Page: It's possible to do a much better job on search, and it's the main application that people use on the Internet. So there's a big opportunity, because if you do a better job, it really matters to people.

Brin: Users may not even realize, but subconsciously, they end up using your search engine because it works better for them. Users end up going where the search is best.

As [we've] watched our traffic grow, time and time again, to beyond capacity, we're really not concerned about [being late to the game].

—*Stern* magazine, January 1999

••

Service as a Goal

Page: Sergey and I founded Google because we believed we could provide an important service to the world—instantly delivering relevant information on virtually any topic. Serving our end users is at the heart of what we do and remains our number one priority.

Our goal is to develop services that significantly improve the lives of as many people as possible.

— "Letter from the Founders" in Amendment 9 to Form S-1, August 18, 2004

••

"Fast is better than slow."

From the Google company website:

We know your time is valuable, so when you're seeking an answer on the Web, you want it right away—and we aim to please. We may be the only people in the world who can say our goal is to have people leave our website as quickly as possible.

—"Ten Things We Know to Be True," Google company website

••

"Focus on the user and all else will follow."

From the Google company website:

Since the beginning, we've focused on providing the best user experience possible. Whether we're designing a new Internet browser or a new tweak to the look of the homepage, we take great care to ensure that they will ultimately serve *you*, rather than our own internal goal or bottom line.

—"Ten Things We Know to Be True,"
Google company website

••

Seamless Product Integration

Page: I have always believed that technology should do the hard work—discovery, organization, communication—so users can do what makes them happiest: living and loving, not messing with annoying computers! That means making our products work together seamlessly. People shouldn't have to navigate Google to get stuff done. It should just happen.

—Google's "2012 Update from the CEO"

••

Simplicity

Page: Our main mission is to organize the world's information and make it universally accessible and useful. It turns out that making the website more complicated doesn't really help with that mission. You basically distract people if you have lots of different things.

—Interview for FT Dynamo, August 6, 2001

••

User Is Never Wrong

Brin: Larry Page and I had a fundamental philosophy when we started Google—the user is never wrong. Other search engine developers would tell us, "That query is too general," or "This query is poorly formed." We try to answer all queries well.

—.com–LIVE, November 4, 1999

••

Personal Information

Brin: People really care about their information. It's their career, it's their health, it's their education.

—Search Engine Watch, 2003

●●

Computer Cookies

Brin: How many people do you think had embarrassing information about them disclosed yesterday because of some [computer] cookie? Zero. It never happens. Yet I'm sure thousands of people had their mail stolen yesterday, or identity theft.

—*New Yorker*, January 14, 2008

Company Culture

....

Scaling

Page: There are strategic issues that keep me up [at night], management issues, organizational issues. As you grow your company, every time you increase by 50 percent it completely changes the culture and the way [you] have to organize.

—Interview for FT Dynamo, August 6, 2001

....

Reorganizing Company Divisions

On reorganizing Google into seven divisions:

Brin: In some ways we have run the company as to let 1,000 flowers bloom, but once they do bloom you want to put together a coherent bouquet.

—Speech at the Web 2.0 Summit, 2011

••

Dogs and Cats

From Google Investor Relations:

Google's affection for our canine friends is an integral facet of our corporate culture. We like cats, but we're a dog company, so as a general rule we feel cats visiting our offices would be fairly stressed out.

—Google Code of Conduct

••

Company Mantra

Brin: As for "Don't be evil," we have tried to define precisely what it means to be a force for good—always to do the right, ethical thing. Ultimately, "Don't be evil" seems the easiest way to summarize it....[But] [i]t's not enough not to be evil. We also actively try to be good.

—*Playboy*, September 2004

. . . .

Startup Mindset

Page: So, since becoming CEO again, I've pushed hard to increase our velocity, improve our execution, and focus on the big bets that will make a difference in the world. Google is a large company now, but we will achieve more, and do it faster, if we approach life with the passion and soul of a startup.

—Google's "2012 Update from the CEO"

. . . .

Company as Family

Page: It's important that the company be a family, that people feel that they're part of the company, and that the company is like a family to them. When you treat people that way, you get better productivity. Rather than caring what hours you worked, you care about output. We should continue to innovate in our relationship with our employees and figure out the best things we can do for them.

—*Fortune*, January 19, 2012

• •

Health Care

Page: [We've been] making sure we have really healthy food for people. We started putting the desserts around a wall, just around the corner. We have doctors on site. We'd like to do more of that, where we really make health care convenient and easy and faster, which I think helps people stay healthy. If your access to health care involves your leaving work and driving somewhere and parking and waiting for a long time, that's not going to promote healthiness.

—*Fortune*, January 19, 2012

• •

Core Areas

Page: It's funny, you'd think you'd run out of things to do in those core areas. But our core areas are so important to people: access to information, understanding the world, communications, interactions with other people, helping you with your work....It's incredibly exciting to come in to work every day and work on those things.

—*Time*, September 30, 2013

Corporate Culture Is Dynamic

Brin: I don't think keeping the culture is a goal. I don't think we should be looking back to our golden years in the garage. The goal is to improve as we grow, and we certainly have more resources to bring to bear on the cultural issues and whatnot as we gain scale.

—*Fortune*, January 31, 2008

Open Communications

From the Google company website:

In our weekly all-hands ("TGIF") meetings—not to mention over email or in the café—Googlers ask questions directly to Larry, Sergey, and other execs about any number of company issues. Our offices and cafés are designed to encourage interactions between Googlers within and across teams, and to spark conversation about work as well as play.

—"Our Culture," Google company website

••

Job Titles

Brin: Titles aren't important. We'll all do better if we have a flat organization with few levels to facilitate communication and avoid bureaucracy.

—I'm Feeling Lucky, 2011

••

"You can be serious without a suit."

From the Google company website:

Our atmosphere may be casual, but as new ideas emerge in a café line, at a team meeting, or at the gym, they are traded, tested, and put into practice with dizzying speed—and they may be the launch pad for a new project destined for worldwide use.

— "Ten Things We Know to Be True,"
Google company website

. . . .

20 Percent Solution

Page and Brin: We encourage our employees, in addition to their regular projects, to spend 20 percent of their time working on what they think will most benefit Google. This empowers them to be more creative and innovative. Many of our significant advances have happened in this manner. For example, AdSense for content and Google News were both prototyped in "20 percent time." Most risky projects fizzle, often teaching us something. Others succeed and become attractive businesses.

—"Letter from the Founders" in Amendment 9 to Form S-1, August 18, 2004

. . . .

Timidity

To in-house engineers:

Page: We wanted something big. Instead, you proposed something small. Why are you so resistant?

—*New Yorker*, January 14, 2008

Leadership

Seeking a CEO

Brin: The model that we look for in a CEO is actually [Amazon.com founder and CEO] Jeff Bezos....Jeff is very smart. Very, very smart. He's a good motivator....I think Larry's probably better than I am [at that], and Jeff is better than he is. That's how we'd rank ourselves. He's definitely very fun to be around, very pleasant to be around, and that's also what you want in a leader at the company, especially since we've worked hard to build a culture.

—"The Lost Google Tapes," January 2000

• •

Larry's Rules of Order

Larry Page's rules of order, as summarized by former Google employee Douglas Edwards:

1. Don't delegate. Do everything you can yourself to make things go faster.
2. Don't get in the way if you're not adding value. Let the people actually doing the work talk to each other while you go do something else. Don't be a bureaucrat.
3. Ideas are more important than age. Just because someone is junior doesn't mean they don't deserve respect and cooperation.
4. The worst thing you can do is stop someone from doing something by saying, "No. Period." If you say no, you have to help them find a better way to get it done.

—*I'm Feeling Lucky*, 2011

••

L-Team

On co-locating top managers, called the L-Team, in an open bullpen of desks:

Page: The insight I got from [former New York City] Mayor [Michael] Bloomberg was that it's maybe more efficient to tell people, "For these hours of the day, we're going to be all together, and at these hours of the day, you're going to be with your team." I'm just trying to get people together for a fixed set of hours in one place.

—*Bloomberg Businessweek*, April 4, 2012

••

The Job of a Leader

Page: My job as a leader is to make sure everybody in the company has great opportunities, and that they feel they're having a meaningful impact and are contributing to the good of society.

—*Fortune*, January 19, 2012

••

Dual CEOs

Page: We're [Brin and Page] basically two in a box. That worked very well for us. [We've spent] an average of 12 hours a day together for the last years we've been working together. We both know what's going on and we're pretty interchangeable. We both respect each other's opinions a lot, so either one of us will make decisions. Usually you have decision paralysis, but we tend to be consistent enough and trust each other enough that we're able to do that.

That allows for much better decisions, because you have two heads instead of one. The CEO is such an important, high-level position. Why not have two people do it? Most peoples' ego gets in the way.

—Interview for FT Dynamo, August 6, 2001

• •

Organizational Challenges

Brin: Probably the most difficult part [of being an entrepreneur] has been learning to deal with organizational challenges. We have over 70 people right now. When it was just a few people it was fine. There weren't any really complicated issues. Now we have a much more complicated yeast. It's not really clear how to keep everybody productive and focused....That's been somewhat of a learning process.

—"The Lost Google Tapes," January 2000

••

Youthful CEO

Page: I think the age is a real issue. It's certainly a handicap in the sense of being able to manage people and to hire people and all these kinds of things, maybe more so than it should be. Certainly, I think, the things that I'm missing are more things that you acquire with time. If you manage people for 20 years or something like that, you pick up things. So I certainly lack experience there, and that's an issue. But I sort of make up for that, I think, in terms of understanding where things are going to go, having a vision about the future, and really understanding the industry I am in, and what the company does, and also sort of the unique position of starting a company and working on it for three years before starting the company. Then working on it pretty hard, whatever, 24 hours a day. So I understand a lot of the aspects pretty well. I guess that compensates a little bit for lack of skills in other areas.

—Interview for Academy of Achievement,
October 28, 2000

•••

"Adult Supervision"

Eric Schmidt was hired as Google's CEO in 2001. When Schmidt stepped down in 2011, he remarked, "Day-to-day adult supervision no longer needed!"

Brin: We're past the age where we're rebellious. You know, earlier, when we were in our teens and so forth, you don't want the parents around. But now we're getting closer to 30 and so forth, and our search engine really serves the world. We perform over 100 million searches a day. It's really important to people. We have a big company—200 employees. It's a large responsibility, and if you can bring in experience to help out, that's pretty reasonable.

—*Charlie Rose*, July 2001

Success and Failure

• •

Ambition

Page: It's often easier to make progress when you're really ambitious. And the reason is that you actually don't have any competition because no one is willing to try those things. And you also get all the best people....Anything you can imagine probably is doable. You just have to imagine it and work on it.

—"Beyond Today," speech at Zeitgeist 2012

• •

Ambition and Failure

Page: Even if you fail at your ambitious thing, it's very hard to fail completely.

—*In the Plex,* 2011

• •

Challenges

Page: I think it is often easier to make progress on mega-ambitious dreams. I know that sounds completely nuts. But since no one else is crazy enough to do it, you have little competition. There are so few people this crazy that I feel like I know them all by first name. They all travel as if they are pack dogs and stick to each other like glue. The best people want to work the big challenges.

—University of Michigan commencement speech,
May 2, 2009

• •

Changing the World

Page: What is the one-sentence summary of how you change the world? Always work hard on something uncomfortably exciting!

—University of Michigan commencement speech,
May 2, 2009

•••

Crazy Ones in Business

Page: [Success is] also a timeliness thing; everyone said Sam Walton was crazy to build big stores in small towns. Almost everyone who has had an idea that's somewhat revolutionary or wildly successful was first told they're insane.

—*Fortune,* May 1, 2008

•••

Internal Risk

Page: Even when we started Google, we thought, "Oh, we might fail," and we almost didn't do it. The reason we started is that Stanford said, "You guys can come back and finish your PhDs if you don't succeed." Probably that one decision caused Google to be created. It's not clear we would have done it otherwise. We had all this internal risk we had just invented. It's not that we were going to starve or not get jobs or not have a good life or whatever, but you have this fear of failing and of doing something new, which is very natural. In order to do stuff that matters, you need to overcome that.

—*Fortune,* May 1, 2008

•••

Fear of Failure

Page: My experience is that when people are trying to do ambitious things, they're all worried about failing when they start. But all sorts of interesting things spin out that are of huge economic value. Also, in these kinds of projects, you get to work with the best people and have a very interesting time. They're not really taking a risk, but they feel like they are.

—*Fortune*, May 1, 2008

•••

Mega-Ambitious Goals

Page: When I was a student at the University of Michigan, I went on a summer leadership course. The slogan was "A healthy disregard for the impossible," and it's an idea that has stayed with me ever since....We've also found that "failed" ambitious projects often yield other dividends.

—Google's "2012 Update from the CEO"

Other Ventures

Optimistic Future

Page: I'm hugely more optimistic, because now we have a conceptualization of the problems that makes some degree of sense to a fair number of people. Look at the things we worry about—poverty, global warming, people dying in accidents. And look at the things that drive people's basic level of happiness—safety and opportunity for their kids, plus basic things like health and shelter. I think our ability to achieve these things on a large scale for many people in the world is improving.

—*Fortune*, May 1, 2008

Philanthropy

Brin: I take the philosophical view that, aside from some modest stuff now, I am waiting to do the bulk of my philanthropy later, maybe in a few years, when I feel I'm more educated. I don't think it's something I have had time to become an expert at.

—*Moment*, February–March 2007

• •

Hybrid Philanthropy

On solar thermal power and other renewable energies:

Page: Our new initiative isn't just about Google's energy needs; we're seeking to accelerate the pace at which clean energy technologies are developing, so they can rival the economics of coal quickly. We've gained expertise in designing and building large-scale, energy-intensive facilities by building data centers that lead the industry in efficiency. We want to apply the same creativity and innovation to the challenge of generating inexpensive renewable electricity at scale....

By combining talented technologists, great partners, and large investments, we have an opportunity to quickly push this technology forward.

—Google Official Blog, November 27, 2007

· ·

Space Tourism

On his $5 million deposit as a "Founding Explorer" of Space Adventures, securing himself a seat on a future spaceflight:

Brin: I am a big believer in the exploration and commercial development of the space frontier, and am looking forward to the possibility of going into space. Space Adventures helped open the space frontier to private citizens and thus pave the way for the personal spaceflight industry. The Orbital Mission Explorers Circle enables me to make an immediate investment while preserving the option to participate in a future spaceflight.

—Space Adventures press release, June 11, 2008

· ·

Aiming High

Page: In some industries it takes 10 or 20 years to go from an idea to something being real. Health care is certainly one of those areas. We should shoot for the things that are really, really important, so 10 or 20 years from now we have those things done.

—*Time,* September 30, 2013

••

$331,450 Hamburger

On investing six figures to create the first test-tube hamburger made of bovine stem cells:

Brin: There are basically three things that can happen going forward. One is we will all become vegetarian—I don't think that's really likely. You know, the second is we ignore the issues, and that leads to continued environmental harm. And the third option is we do something new.

Some people think this is science fiction—it's not real; it's somewhere out there. I actually think that's a good thing. If what you are doing is not seen by some people as science fiction, it's probably not transformative enough.

It's really just a proof of concept right now. We're trying to create the first cultured beef hamburger; from there, I'm optimistic we can really scale by leaps and bounds.

—"Introducing Cultured Beef," Maastricht University Cultured Beef/Department of Expansion

Calico, Google's Health-Care Initiative

Page: You're probably thinking, Wow! That's a lot different from what Google does today. And you're right. But as we explained in our first letter to shareholders, there's tremendous potential for technology more generally to improve people's lives. So don't be surprised if we invest in projects that seem strange or speculative compared with our existing Internet businesses. And please re-member that new investments like this are very small by comparison to our core business.

....[Aging and illness] affect us all—from the decreased mobility and mental agility that comes with age, to life-threatening diseases that exact a terrible physical and emotional toll on individuals and families. And while this is clearly a longer-term bet, we believe we can make good progress within reasonable timescales with the right goals and the right people.

—Personal post on Google+, September 18, 2013

....

Genetic Predisposition for Parkinson's Disease

Brin: I know early in my life something I am substantially predisposed to. I now have the opportunity to adjust my life to reduce those odds (e.g., there is evidence that exercise may be protective against Parkinson's). I also have the opportunity to perform and support research into this disease long before it may affect me. And, regardless of my own health, it can help my family members as well as others.

I feel fortunate to be in this position. Until the fountain of youth is discovered, all of us will have some conditions in our old age—only we don't know what they will be. I have a better guess than almost anyone else for what ills may be mine—and I have decades to prepare for it.

—*Too* (personal blog), September 18, 2008

Mars—or Bust!

From an April Fools' joke, which included a website promoting the idea of populating a Mars colony called "Virgle City" by 2108. (Virgin's Sir Richard Branson added, "Some people are calling Virgle an 'interplanetary Noah's Ark. I'm one of them. It's a potentially remarkable business, but more than that, it's a glorious adventure. For me, Virgle evokes the spirit of explorers such as Christopher Columbus and Marco Polo, who set sail looking for the New World. I do hope we'll be a bit more efficient about actually finding it, though."):

Brin: We're here to tell you about Project Virgle. It's the first human settlement on the planet Mars, and this is the biggest endeavor we have ever undertaken at Google and at Virgin. We're going to select the very first settlers of the planet Mars.

Page: And to do that, we're encouraging you all to submit a 30-second YouTube video, which Sergey's gonna look at personally.

Brin: I might not get a chance to look through all of them, but we're both definitely gonna review all the finalists, and if you're chosen, you're gonna get to join Larry, Richard [Branson], and myself on the planet Mars sometime in the next 20 years.

—"Larry Page and Sergey Brin on Virgle,"
April 1, 2008

Life Lessons

....

Dreams

Page: You never lose a dream; it just incubates as a hobby.

—University of Michigan commencement speech,
May 2, 2009

....

Family as Priority

Page: Many of us are fortunate enough to be here with family. Some of us have dear friends and family to go home to. And who knows, perhaps some of you, like Lucy and I, are dreaming about future families of your own. Just like me, your families brought you here, and you brought them here. Please keep them close and remember: They are what really matters in life.

—University of Michigan commencement speech,
May 2, 2009

....

Feynman, Theoretical Physicist

Brin: I remember really enjoying [Richard] Feynman's books. He had several autobiographical books, and I read them. It seemed like a very great life he led. Aside from making really big contributions in his own field, he was pretty broadminded. I remember he had an excerpt where he was explaining how he really wanted to be a Leonardo, an artist and a scientist. I found that pretty inspiring. I think that leads to having a fulfilling life.

—Interview for Academy of Achievement,
October 28, 2000

....

Frugality

Brin: From my parents, I certainly learned to be frugal and to be happy without very many things. It's interesting—I still find myself not wanting to leave anything on the plate uneaten. I still look at prices. I try to force myself to do this less, not to be so frugal. But I was raised being happy with not so much.

—*Moment*, February–March 2007

• •

Great Expectations

In a speech to a group of gifted students at a high school near Tel Aviv:

Brin: I have standard Russian-Jewish parents. My dad is a math professor. They have a certain attitude about studies. And I think I can relate that here, because I was told your school recently got seven out of the top ten places in a math competition throughout all Israel. What I have to say is, in the words of my father: "What about the other three?"

— Speech to Israeli students, September 2003

• •

Goal Setting

Page: You have to be a little silly about the goals you are going to set....You should try to do things most people would not.

— Speech to Israeli students, September 2003

••

Growing Up in the United States, and Not Russia

Brin: I think, if anything, I've...gotten a gift by being in the States rather than growing up in Russia...it just makes me appreciate my life much more.

—Interview for Academy of Achievement, October 28, 2000

••

Meetings

Page: It's amazing how few people in positions of power have a deep technical or scientific background. I have a theory about this, which is, it basically has to do with meetings. We try actually very hard to get our engineers to come to meetings at Google and they never do; they just refuse. They just sort of run screaming back to their computer[s]. Actually, it's true for me to some extent too. I really don't like going to meetings, but I've fought it and now I've overcome that issue and I can do that, and that's a very important skill to have.

—Address at the American Association for the Advancement of Science, February 2007

•••

Steve Jobs

Page: He always seemed to be able to say in very few words what you actually should have been thinking before you thought it. His focus on the user experience above all else has always been an inspiration to me.

—Personal post on Google+, October 5, 2011

•••

Striking Employees

Page: My grandfather worked in the auto plants in Flint, Michigan. He was an assembly-line worker. During the sit-down strikes he used to carry this long iron pipe with a big chunk of lead on the end when he walked to work....[t]o protect himself from the company. I still have the hammer. That's two generations ago, and we've come a long way. I don't think any of our employees have to carry such weapons to work. At least I hope they don't. But that's a big change in two generations. It's common sense: Happy people are more productive.

—*Time*, January 29, 2008

••

Wealth

Brin: It takes a lot of getting used to. You always hear the phrase "Money doesn't buy you happiness." But I always, in the back of my mind, figured a lot of money will buy you a little bit of happiness. But it's not really true. I got a new car because the old one's lease expired. Nothing terribly fancy—you could drive the same car.

—*Time*, February 20, 2006

••

Working 24/7

Page: I think it definitely helps to be really focused on what you are doing. You can only work so many hours, and I try to have some balance in my life and so on. I think a lot of people go through this in school. They work really hard. You can do that for part of your life, but you can't do that indefinitely. At some point, you want to have a family. You want to have more time to do other things. I would say that is an advantage of being young. You don't have as many other responsibilities.

—Interview for Academy of Achievement,
October 28, 2000

••

Standing Up for Your Principles

Brin: I think at some point it is appropriate to stand up for your principles, and if more companies, governments, [and] individuals did that, I do think the world would be a better place.

—Sergey Brin and Larry Page:
Founders of Google, 2010

EXCERPTS FROM 2004 FOUNDERS' LETTER

From the S-1 Registration Statement

"An Owner's Manual" for Google's Shareholders[1]

Introduction

Google is not a conventional company. We do not intend to become one. Throughout Google's evolution as a privately held company, we have managed Google differently. We have also emphasized an atmosphere of creativity and challenge, which has helped us provide unbiased, accurate and free access to information for those who rely on us around the world.

---

[1] Much of this was inspired by Warren Buffett's essays in his annual reports and his "An Owner's Manual" to Berkshire Hathaway shareholders.

Now the time has come for the company to move to public ownership. This change will bring important benefits for our employees, for our present and future shareholders, for our customers, and most of all for Google users. But the standard structure of public ownership may jeopardize the independence and focused objectivity that have been most important in Google's past success and that we consider most fundamental for its future. Therefore, we have implemented a corporate structure that is designed to protect Google's ability to innovate and retain its most distinctive characteristics. We are confident that, in the long run, this will benefit Google and its shareholders, old and new. We want to clearly explain our plans and the reasoning and values behind them. We are delighted you are considering an investment in Google and are reading this letter....

Serving End Users

Sergey and I founded Google because we believed we could provide an important service to the world—instantly delivering relevant information on virtually any topic. Serving our end users is at the heart of what we do and remains our number one priority.

Our goal is to develop services that significantly improve the lives of as many people as possible. In pursuing this goal, we may do things that we believe have a positive impact on the world, even if the near term financial returns are not obvious. For example, we make our services as widely available as we can by supporting over 90 languages and by providing most services for free. Advertising is our principal source of revenue, and the ads we provide are relevant and useful rather than intrusive and annoying. We strive to provide users with great commercial information.

We are proud of the products we have built, and we hope that those we create in the future will have an even greater positive impact on the world.

Long Term Focus

As a private company, we have concentrated on the long term, and this has served us well. As a public company, we will do the same. In our opinion, outside pressures too often tempt companies to sacrifice long term opportunities to meet quarterly market expectations. Sometimes this pressure has caused companies to manipulate financial results in order to "make their quarter." In Warren Buffett's words, "We won't 'smooth' quarterly or annual results: If earnings figures are lumpy when they reach headquarters, they will be lumpy when they reach you."

If opportunities arise that might cause us to sacrifice short term results but are in the best long term interest of our shareholders, *we will take those opportunities*. We will have the fortitude to do this. We would request that our shareholders take the long term view.

You might ask how long is long term? Usually we expect projects to have some realized benefit or progress within a year or two. But, we are trying to look forward as far as we can. Despite the quickly changing business and technology landscape, we try to look at three- to five-year scenarios in order to decide what to do now. We try to optimize total benefit over these multi-year scenarios. While we are strong advocates of this strategy, it is difficult to make good multi-year predictions in technology.

Many companies are under pressure to keep their earnings in line with analysts' forecasts. Therefore, they often accept smaller, predictable earnings rather than larger and less predictable returns. Sergey and I feel this is harmful, and we intend to steer in the opposite direction.

Google has had adequate cash to fund our business and has generated additional cash through operations. This gives us the flexibility to weather costs, benefit from opportunities and optimize our long term earnings. For example, in our ads system we make many improvements that affect revenue in both directions. These are in areas like end user relevance and satisfaction, advertiser satisfaction, partner needs and targeting technology. We release improvements immediately rather than delaying them, even though delay might give "smoother" financial results. You have our commitment to execute quickly to achieve long term value rather than making the quarters more predictable.

Our long term focus does have risks. Markets may have trouble evaluating long term value, thus potentially reducing the value of our company. Our long term focus may simply be the wrong business strategy. Competitors may be rewarded for short term tactics and grow stronger as a result. As potential investors, you should consider the risks around our long term focus.

We will make business decisions with the long term welfare of our company and shareholders in mind and not based on accounting considerations.

Although we may discuss long term trends in our business, we do not plan to give earnings guidance in the traditional sense. We are not able to predict our business within a narrow range for each quarter. We recognize that our duty is to advance our shareholders' interests, and we believe that artificially creating short term target numbers serves our shareholders poorly. We would prefer not to be asked to make such predictions, and if asked we will respectfully decline. A management team distracted by a series of short term targets is as pointless as a dieter stepping on a scale every half hour.

Risk vs. Reward in the Long Run

Our business environment changes rapidly and needs long term investment. We will not hesitate to place major bets on promising new opportunities.

We will not shy away from high-risk, high-reward projects because of short term earnings pressure. Some of our past bets have gone extraordinarily well, and others have not. Because we recognize the pursuit of such projects as the key to our long term success, we will continue to seek them out. For example, we would fund projects that have a 10% chance of earning a billion dollars over the long term. Do not be surprised if we place smaller bets in areas that seem very speculative or even strange when compared to our current businesses. Although we cannot quantify the specific level of risk we will undertake, as the ratio of reward to risk increases, we will accept projects further outside our current businesses, especially when the initial investment is small relative to the level of investment in our current businesses.

We encourage our employees, in addition to their regular projects, to spend 20% of their time working on what they think will most benefit Google. This empowers them to be more creative and innovative. Many of our significant advances have happened in this manner. For example, Ad-Sense for content and Google News were both prototyped in "20% time." Most risky projects fizzle, often teaching us something. Others succeed and become attractive businesses.

As we seek to maximize value in the long term, we may have quarter-to-quarter volatility as we realize losses on some new projects and gains on others. We would love to better quantify our level of risk and reward for you going forward, but that is very difficult. Even though we are excited about risky projects, we expect to devote the vast majority of our resources to improvements to our main businesses (currently search and advertising). Most employees naturally gravitate toward incremental improvements in core areas so this tends to happen naturally.

Executive Roles[2]

We run Google as a triumvirate. Sergey and I have worked closely together for the last eight years, five at Google. Eric, our CEO, joined Google three years ago. The three of us run the company collaboratively with Sergey and me as Presidents. The structure is

---

[2] Editor's note: The current lineup of executive positions: Larry Page is the CEO; he was formerly the president of products from 2001 to 2011. Eric E. Schmidt is the Executive Chairman; he was formerly the CEO from 2001 to 2011. Sergey Brin directs special projects; he was formerly president of technology from 2001 to 2011.

unconventional, but we have worked successfully in this way.

To facilitate timely decisions, Eric, Sergey and I meet daily to update each other on the business and to focus our collaborative thinking on the most important and immediate issues. Decisions are often made by one of us, with the others being briefed later. This works because we have tremendous trust and respect for each other and we generally think alike. Because of our intense long term working relationship, we can often predict differences of opinion among the three of us. We know that when we disagree, the correct decision is far from obvious. For important decisions, we discuss the issue with a larger team appropriate to the task. Differences are resolved through discussion and analysis and by reaching consensus. Eric, Sergey and I run the company without any significant internal conflict, but with healthy debate. As different topics come up, we often delegate decision-making responsibility to one of us.

We hired Eric as a more experienced complement to Sergey and me to help us run the business. Eric was CTO of Sun Microsystems. He was also CEO of Novell and has a PhD in computer science, a very unusual and important combination for Google given our scientific and technical culture. This partnership among the three of us has worked very well and we expect it to continue. The shared judgments and extra energy available from all three of us has significantly benefited Google.

Eric has the legal responsibilities of the CEO and focuses on management of our vice presidents and the sales organization. Sergey focuses on engineering and business deals. I focus on engineering and product management. All three of us devote considerable time to overall management of the company and other fluctuating needs. We also have a distinguished board of directors to oversee the management of Google. We have a talented executive staff that manages day-to-day operations in areas such as finance, sales, engineering, human resources, public relations, legal and product management. We are extremely fortunate to have talented management that has grown the company to where it is today—they operate the company and deserve the credit.

Corporate Structure

We are creating a corporate structure that is designed for stability over long time horizons. By investing in Google, you are placing an unusual long term bet on the team, especially Sergey and me, and on our innovative approach.

We want Google to become an important and significant institution. That takes time, stability and independence. We bridge the media and technology industries, both of which have experienced considerable consolidation and attempted hostile takeovers.

In the transition to public ownership, we have set up a corporate structure that will make it harder for outside parties to take over or influence Google. This structure will also make it easier for our management team to follow the long term, innovative approach emphasized earlier. This structure, called a dual class voting structure, is described elsewhere in this prospectus. The Class A common stock we are offering has one vote per share, while the Class B common stock held by many current shareholders has 10 votes per share.

The main effect of this structure is likely to leave our team, especially Sergey and me, with increasingly significant control over the company's decisions and fate, as Google shares change hands. After the IPO, Sergey, Eric and I will control 37.6% of the voting power of Google, and the executive management team and directors as a group will control 61.4% of the voting power. New investors will fully share in Google's long term economic future but will have little ability to influence its strategic decisions through their voting rights.

While this structure is unusual for technology companies, similar structures are common in the media business and have had a profound importance there. The New York Times Company, The Washington Post Company and Dow Jones, the publisher of *The Wall Street Journal*, all have similar dual class ownership structures. Media observers have pointed out that dual class ownership has allowed these companies to concentrate on their core, long term interest in serious news coverage, despite fluctuations in quarterly results. Berkshire Hathaway has implemented a dual class structure for similar reasons. From the point of view of long term success in advancing a company's core values, we believe this structure has clearly been an advantage.

Some academic studies have shown that from a purely economic point of view, dual class structures have not harmed the share price of companies. Other studies have concluded that dual class structures have negatively affected share prices, and we cannot assure you that this will not be the case with Google. The shares of each of our classes have identical economic rights and differ only as to voting rights....

IPO Pricing and Allocation

It is important to us to have a fair process for our IPO that is inclusive of both small and large investors. It is also crucial that we achieve a good out-

come for Google and its current shareholders. This has led us to pursue an auction-based IPO for our entire offering. Our goal is to have a share price that reflects an efficient market valuation of Google that moves rationally based on changes in our business and the stock market....

We would like you to invest for the long term, and you should not expect to sell Google shares for a profit shortly after Google's IPO. We encourage investors not to invest in Google at IPO or for some time after, if they believe the price is not sustainable over the long term. Even in the long term, the trading price of Google's stock may decline....

Googlers

Our employees, who have named themselves Googlers, are everything. Google is organized around the ability to attract and leverage the talent of exceptional technologists and business people. We have been lucky to recruit many creative, principled and hard working stars. We hope to recruit many more in the future. We will reward and treat them well.

We provide many unusual benefits for our employees, including meals free of charge, doctors and washing machines. We are careful to consider the long term advantages to the company of these benefits. Expect us to add benefits rather than pare them down over time. We believe it is easy to be penny wise and pound foolish with respect to benefits that can save employees considerable time and improve their health and productivity.

The significant employee ownership of Google has made us what we are today. Because of our employee talent, Google is doing exciting work in nearly every area of computer science. We are in a very competitive industry where the quality of our product is paramount. Talented people are attracted to Google because we empower them to change the world; Google has large computational resources and distribution that enables individuals to make a difference. Our main benefit is a workplace with important projects, where employees can contribute and grow. We are focused on providing an environment where talented, hard working people are rewarded for their contributions to Google and for making the world a better place.

Don't Be Evil

Don't be evil. We believe strongly that in the long term, we will be better served—as shareholders and in all other ways—by a company that does good things for the world even if we forgo some short term gains. This is an important aspect of our culture and is broadly shared within the company.

Google users trust our systems to help them with important decisions: medical, financial and many others. Our search results are the best we know how to produce. They are unbiased and objective, and we do not accept payment for them or for inclusion or more frequent updating. We also display advertising, which we work hard to make relevant, and we label it clearly. This is similar to a well-run newspaper, where the advertisements are clear and the articles are not influenced by the advertisers' payments. We believe it is important for everyone to have access to the best information and research, not only to the information people pay for you to see.

Making the World a Better Place

We aspire to make Google an institution that makes the world a better place. In pursuing this goal, we will always be mindful of our responsibilities to our shareholders, employees, customers and business partners. With our products, Google connects people and information all around the world for free. We are adding other powerful services such as Gmail, which provides an efficient one gigabyte Gmail account for free. We know that some people have raised privacy concerns, primarily over Gmail's targeted ads, which could lead to negative perceptions about Google. However, we believe Gmail protects a user's privacy. By releasing services, such as Gmail, for free, we hope to help bridge the digital divide. AdWords connects users and advertisers efficiently, helping both. AdSense helps fund a huge variety of online websites and enables authors who could not otherwise publish. Last year we created Google Grants—a growing program in which hundreds of non-profits addressing issues, including the environment, poverty and human rights, receive free advertising. And now, we are in the process of establishing the Google Foundation. We intend to contribute significant resources to the foundation, including employee time and approximately 1% of Google's equity and profits in some form. We hope someday this institution may eclipse Google itself in terms of overall world impact by ambitiously applying innovation and significant resources to the largest of the world's problems.

Summary and Conclusion

Google is not a conventional company. Eric, Sergey and I intend to operate Google differently, applying the values it has developed as a private company to its future as a public company. Our mission and business description are available in the rest of this prospectus; we encourage you to carefully read this information. We will optimize for the long term rather than trying to produce smooth earnings for each quarter. We will support selected high-risk, high-reward projects and manage our portfolio of projects. We will run the company collaboratively with Eric, our CEO, as a team of three. We are conscious of our duty as fiduciaries for our shareholders, and we will fulfill those responsibilities. We will continue to strive to attract creative, committed new employees, and we will welcome support from new shareholders. We will live up to our "don't be evil" principle by keeping user trust and not accepting payment for search results. We have a dual class structure that is biased toward stability and independence and that requires investors to bet on the team, especially Sergey and me.

In this letter we have talked about our IPO auction method and our desire for stability and access for all investors. We have discussed our goal to have investors who invest for the long term. Finally, we have discussed our desire to create an ideal working environment that will ultimately drive the success of Google by retaining and attracting talented Googlers.

We have tried hard to anticipate your questions. It will be difficult for us to respond to them given legal constraints during our offering process. We look forward to a long and hopefully prosperous relationship with you, our new investors. We wrote this letter to help you understand our company.

We have a strong commitment to our users worldwide, their communities, the websites in our network, our advertisers, our investors, and of course our employees. Sergey and I, and the team will do our best to make Google a long term success and the world a better place.

Larry Page   **Sergey Brin**

MILESTONES

1973

March 26: Lawrence Page is born in East Lansing, Michigan, to Gloria and Carl Page. (His parents taught computer science at Michigan State University.)

August 21: Sergey Mikhaylovich Brin is born in Moscow, Russia, to Eugenia and Michael Brin. (His parents are graduates of Moscow State University. His father taught math at the University of Maryland; his mother was a researcher at NASA's Goddard Space Flight Center.)

1975

September: Page enrolls in the Okemos Montessori School (now Montessori Radmoor), which he attends until 1979.

1979

October: Brin and his family emigrate from Russia to the United States to escape Jewish persecution.

1991

June: Page graduates from East Lansing High School.

1993

May: Brin graduates with a BS from the University of Maryland.

1995

Page and Brin meet on the campus of Stanford University, when Brin is assigned to show Page, who is considering attending its graduate program, around campus.

May: Page graduates with a BA from the University of Michigan's College of Engineering.

June: Brin graduates with an MS from Stanford University.

1996

Page and Brin collaborate on a Web search engine called BackRub, which would later be renamed Google (for "googol," the number 1 followed by 100 zeros). The name is properly suggestive of the massive scope of what they intend to accomplish: cataloging and updating every page on the World Wide Web.

1997

Page and Brin discard BackRub and adopt "Google" as the search engine's official name.

1998

June: Page graduates with an MS from Stanford University.

August: Google is initially funded for $100,000 by Andy Bechtolsheim, although the company does not yet formally exist. (The check, made out to "Google Inc.," could not be cashed until a lawyer set it up as a corporation.)

September: Google rents space at a suburban home owned by Susan Wojcicki; its address is 232 Santa Margarita Avenue, Menlo Park, California.

Google formally incorporates on September 4.

Brin and Page deposit Bechtolsheim's initial funding check.

Google hires its first employee (Craig Silverstein), a fellow computer science grad student at Stanford.

1999

February: Google, with eight employees, moves to an office building at 165 University Avenue in Palo Alto.

April: Google, a canine-friendly company, sees its first dog come to the office. Thereafter, employees' dogs are allowed to come to work—but no cats.

June: Google receives its first major funding from Sequoia Capital and Kleiner Perkins, for $25 million.

August: Google expands, needing more space, and moves to 2400 E. Bayshore in Mountain View, California.

November: Google hires its first full-time chef. The café (*not* cafeteria) offers free, nutritious food to all employees, keeping them on-site and working instead of leaving the campus.

2000

Google becomes the world's largest search engine, with 1 billion Web pages indexed.

April: Google's first April Fools' joke is sprung on an unsuspecting world. It becomes a company tradition.

October: Google, which has thus far rejected traditional Web advertising vehicles like banners and paid placement ads, launches AdWords (targeted ads based on search engine queries). The revolutionary advertising vehicle carries the day: It will account for the majority of Google's revenue in the years to come.

2001

March: Google hires Dr. Eric Schmidt, then chairman and CEO of Novell, Inc., as its board chairman.

August: Schmidt takes the helm as CEO, succeeding Page, who says in a press release dated August 6 that Schmidt's "extensive technology background and vision for the potential of the Internet complement the efforts that Google is making in defining a leadership position in Internet search and navigation. His strong management experience will help shape Google as we continue our growth and global expansion. And most importantly for anyone taking on the CEO role at Google, Eric is a natural fit with our corporate culture." Google now has, as Sergey Brin put it, "day-to-day adult supervision" (a reference to a 2001 interview on *Charlie Rose*, in which Rose asked, "...you guys couldn't run it yourself?" and Brin responded, "Parental supervision, to be honest." When Rose asked if they needed "adult supervision," Page responded, "I don't know if I'd say *need*, but it's really nice to have.")

2003

December: Google Print (later renamed Google Books) is launched.

2004

February: Larry Page is inducted into the National Academy of Engineering "for the creation of the Google search engine."

March: Google moves to 1600 Amphitheatre Parkway in Mountain View, called the "Googleplex," a campus-like environment conducive to work and play.

August: Google's IPO goes on the market at $85 a share. The initial offering of Class A common stock is 19,605,052 shares.

October: The Marconi Society names Page and Brin as Fellows, affirming their "lasting scientific contributions to human progress in the field of communications science and the Internet." As Google Fellow Urs Hölzle points out in an official Google blog entry dated October 22, "Those of us who are lucky enough to make our living thinking about challenging problems know that real breakthroughs are rarely as discontinuous as they might appear. Sometimes it's a matter of timing. Sometimes it's a matter of two failed approaches coming together with a twist that makes them right. So when we win recognition for what Google has become, we like to remind ourselves that many others have contributed to our success. As Newton said, 'If I have seen farther than others, it is because I have stood on the shoulders of giants.'"

2005

June: Google's Mobile Web Search is released.

2006

February: Dr. Eric Schmidt is inducted into the National Academy of Engineering.

June: Google Checkout (replaced by Google Wallet in 2013), an alternative to online payment companies like PayPal, is rolled out.

The *Oxford English Dictionary* adds "google" to its pages as a verb. The OED defines it as: "*intr.* to use the Google search engine to find information on the Internet. *trans.* To enter (a search term) into the Google search engine to find information on the Internet; to search for information about (a person or thing) using the Google search engine."

October: Google pays $1.65 billion in stock for YouTube.

2007

November: Google announces Android, an open platform OS for mobile devices. (In 2013, it would claim 81 percent market share. Apple CEO Tim Cook, in *Bloomberg Businessweek*, September 19, 2013, disparages Android as a cheaper, inferior alternative to its iPhone: "There's always a large junk part of the market. We're not in the junk business....I'm not going to lose sleep over that other market, because it's just not who we are.")

2008

Google releases its Chrome browser, initially for Microsoft Windows only.

July: Google indexes one trillion pages, according to its official blog.

September: T-Mobile announces the first cell phone using the Android OS—the G1. Unlike the Apple OS, the Android OS is open source. In a Google blog entry dated September 23, Google's Erick Tseng, lead project manager for the Android team, explains, "Everyone will be free to adopt and adapt the technology as they see fit. By doing so, we hope that users will get better, more capable phones with powerful Web browsers and access to a rich catalogue of innovative mobile applications."

2009

December: Google releases its Chrome browser for the Mac and Linux platforms.

2010

February: Google announces its high-speed broadband networks, which are 100 times faster than what American consumers currently use. Cities will include Kansas City, Kansas; Kansas City, Missouri, and other KC suburbs; Austin, Texas; and Provo, Utah. (More than 1,000 communities applied to be carriers.)

May: Google invests in its first renewable energy project—two wind farms generating 169.5 megawatts of power.

2011

January: Google announces a major management shakeup: Page will assume CEO duties in April, and Schmidt will become Google's Executive Chairman.

May: Google determines that its AdWords sales generated $64 billion in economic impact, assuming that every dollar spent on AdWords generates $8 in profit via AdWords and Google Search.

September: Google Wallet debuts, allowing electronic payments by cell phone.

2012

April: Google shows off its Project Glass, a wearable computer in the form of eyeglasses costing $1,500 a pair. Ten thousand people tried out an early version as part of a contest. (As a Google spokesperson told *The Verge*, "It's certainly early days of the device—there will be bumps. But what's cool is that we're approach-

ing the time when people will be able to take Glass
out into the world and start exploring what's possible
with a device like this.") Early adopters are dubbed
"Glass Explorers" by Google; its critics, however, call
them "glassholes."

September: Google indexes 50 billion pages, according to
Data Center Knowledge.

October: Google releases the Chromebook, a "Cloud-
only" laptop for $249, with built-in Google products
and thousands of free apps.

2013

February: Google announces the Chromebook Pixel, the
second iteration of its Chromebook, for $1,299 and
$1,449.

August: A spokesman for Brin and his wife, Anne
Wojcicki, confirms reports that they are separated.

September: Google celebrates its 15th birthday.

October: Google stock breaks the $1,000-per-share
price.

2014

April 5: Google stock splits, creating Class C nonvoting
shares.

April 15: Google offers its wearable Google Glass for sale
for one day, at $1,500 a pair, and sells out of its initial
allotment.

April 18: Current share price is $536.10. The company has
a market capitalization of $363.39 billion.

But like I said, I'm motivated to make Google into something even more amazing and have a really tremendous positive impact on the world ultimately.

We're still 1 percent to where we should be. I feel a deep sense of responsibility to try to move things along. Not enough people are focused on big change. Part of what I'm trying to do is take Google as a case study and really scale our ambition such that we are able to cause more positive change in the world and more technological change. I have a deep feeling that we are not even close to where we should be.

—LARRY PAGE ON GOOGLE'S FUTURE,
FORTUNE, 2012

CITATIONS

Introduction

"The greatest crisis facing us is…": Robert A. Heinlein,
"Where To?," *Expanded Universe: The New Worlds of
Robert A. Heinlein*, 1980. New York: Ace Books.

"Actually, more and more librarians …": David
Sheff, "Playboy Interview: Google Guys," *Playboy*,
September 2004.

Early Years

Family's First Computer

Verne Kopytoff, "Larry Page's Connections: A
Conversation with Chronicle Staff Writer Verne
Kopytoff," *San Francisco Chronicle*, December 31,
2000.
http://www.sfgate.com/business/article/Larry-Page-s
-Connections-A-conversation-with-3236053.php.

Stanford University

John Battelle, *The Search: How Google and Its Rivals
Rewrote the Rules of Business and Transformed Our
Culture*, 2005. New York: Penguin Group.
Kindle edition.

Academia

Sergey Brin and Larry Page interview for Academy of
Achievement, London, October 28, 2000. http://www
.achievement.org/autodoc/page/pagoint-1.

Serendipity

"Corporate Valley Presents: Exclusive Interview of Larry
Page and Sergey Brin" (video), January 24, 2013.
http://www.youtube.com/watch?v=0vvoNKieCoI.

Following Dreams

Larry Page, University of Michigan commencement
speech, May 2, 2009. http://googlepress.blogspot
.com/2009/05/larry-pages-university-of-michigan.html.

Business Opportunity

Ben Elgin, "Online Extra: Google's Goal: 'Understand
Everything,'" *Bloomberg Businessweek*, May 2, 2004.
http://www.businessweek.com/stories/2004-05-02
/online-extra-googles-goal-understand-everything.

Initial Funding

"The Lost Google Tapes," Sergey Brin and Larry Page
interview with John F. Ince, January 2000, quoted in
John F. Ince, "The Lost Tapes: Conversations Tape-
Recorded in the Early Years With Google's Founders
Illuminate How Their Actions Forged the Growth
of a Silicon Valley Giant," *San Francisco Chronicle*,
December 3, 2006.
http://www.sfgate.com/opinion/article/THE-LOST
-TAPES-Conversations-tape-recorded-in-2544534
.php#photo-2640696.

Celebrating Funding

John Battelle, *The Search: How Google and Its Rivals
Rewrote the Rules of Business and Transformed Our
Culture*, 2005. New York: Penguin Group.
Kindle edition.

Work Hours

Karsten Lemm, "Hier Völlig in Ordnung," *Stern* magazine, January 1999. http://www.ubergizmo.com/2008/09/googles-first-steps/.

Growth of Google

Adam Tanner, "Google Founders Have Grown Up, CEO says," *Reuters*, May 9, 2008. http://mobile.reuters.com/article/businessNews/idUSN0841778920080508?src=RSS-BUS.

Products and Technology

Scope of Google

Sergey Brin and Larry Page interview for Academy of Achievement, London, October 28, 2000. http://www.achievement.org/autodoc/page/pagoint-1.

Better Search Engine

University of Michigan College of Engineering, "Larry Page," *Michigan Engineer*, Spring/Summer 2001. http://www.eecs.umich.edu/eecs/alumni/Stories/Page_coe.html.

Artificial Intelligence

Larry Page, address at the American Association for the Advancement of Science, San Francisco, February 2007. http://www.abc.net.au/radionational/programs/scienceshow/changing-the-world---larry-page/3394966#transcript.

Ideal Searcher

Sergey Brin interview for *.com–LIVE* by Leslie Walker, *Washington Post*, November 4, 1999. http://www.washingtonpost.com/wp-srv/liveonline/business/walker/walker110499.htm.

Perfect Search Engine

Jason Pontin, "Dinner With the Mind Behind the Mind of God: A Meeting with Sergey Brin, Cofounder of Google, at the Russian Tea Room in San Francisco," *Red Herring*, July 16, 2002.

Design

Larry Page, Google's 2013 Q2 earnings call, quoted in Farhad Manjoo, "Google: The Redesign," *Fast Company*, October 2013. http://www.fastcodesign.com/3016268/google-the-redesign.

Google as Reference Librarian

Ben Elgin, "Online Extra: Google's Goal: 'Understand Everything,'" *Bloomberg Businessweek*, May 2, 2004. http://www.businessweek.com/stories/2004-05-02/online-extra-googles-goal-understand-everything.

Books Online

Jefferson Graham, "Google to Sell Books to Be Read Only Online," *USA Today*, October 28, 2008. http://usatoday30.usatoday.com/tech/news/2008-10-28-google-lawsuit_n.htm.

Google Books

Google, "Authors, Publishers, and Google Reach Landmark Settlement: Copyright Accord Would Make Millions More Books Available Online" (press release), October 28, 2008. http://googlepress.blogspot .com/2008/10/authors-publishers-and-google -reach_28.html.

Google Glass

Sergey Brin, "Why Google Glass?," *TED Talks* (video), February 2013. http://www.ted.com/talks/sergey_brin _why_google_glass.html.

"I'm Feeling Lucky" Option for Google's Search Engine

Brendan Newnam, "Are You Feeling Lucky? Google Is," *Marketplace*, November 19, 2007. http://www.marketplace.org/topics/world /are-you-feeling-lucky-google.

"Jew Watch" Website

Mark Malseed, "The Story of Sergey Brin," *Moment*, February–March 2007. http://www.momentmag.com /the-story-of-sergey-brin/.

Products

Steven Levy, "Google's Larry Page on Why Moon Shots Matter," *Wired*, January 17, 2013. http://www.wired .com/business/2013/01/ff-qa-larry-page/.

Self-Driving Cars

Larry Page, "Beyond Today," speech at Zeitgeist 2012 (video). https://www.youtube.com/watch?v=YoWH -CoFwn4.

Smartphones

Larry Page, "Beyond Today," speech at Zeitgeist 2012 (video). https://www.youtube.com/watch?v=YoWH-CoFwn4.

Think Crazy

Larry Page, Q & A at Zeitgeist Americas 2012 (video). https://www.youtube.com/watch?v=4Mzlp6mIaC4.

Think Long Term

Larry Page, "2012 Update from the CEO," Google Investor Relations. http://investor.google.com/corporate/2012/ceo-letter.html.

Moon Shots

Harry McCracken and Lev Grossman, "The Audacity of Google: Larry Page and the Art of the Moon Shot," *Time*, September 30, 2013.

Toothbrush Test

Larry Page, "Beyond Today," speech at Zeitgeist 2012 (video). https://www.youtube.com/watch?v=YoWH-CoFwn4.

Mission of Google

Sergey Brin and Larry Page interview for Academy of Achievement, London, October 28, 2000. http://www.achievement.org/autodoc/page/pagoint-1.

Innovation and Competition

Competitors

Brad Stone, "Google's Page: Apple's Android Pique 'For Show,'" *Bloomberg Businessweek*, April 4, 2012.

http://www.businessweek.com/articles/2012-04-04
/googles-page-apples-android-pique-for-show.

Big Bets

Steven Levy, "Google's Larry Page on Why Moon Shots
Matter," *Wired*, January 17, 2013. http://www.wired
.com/business/2013/01/ff-qa-larry-page/.

Multiple Goals

Harry McCracken and Lev Grossman, "The Audacity of
Google: Larry Page and the Art of the Moon Shot,"
Time, September 30, 2013.

70/20/10

Andy Serwer, "Larry Page on How to Change the World,"
Fortune, May 1, 2008. http://money.cnn
.com/2008/04/29/magazines/fortune
/larry_page_change_the_world.fortune/index.htm.

"Great just isn't good enough."

"Ten Things We Know to Be True," Google company
website. www.google.com/about/company
/philosophy.

Fast Decision-Making

Larry Page, Q & A with Eric Schmidt at Zeitgeist
Americas 2011 (video). https://www.youtube.com
/watch?v=srI6QYfi-HY.

Dot-com Zeitgeist

David Sheff, "Playboy Interview: Google Guys," *Playboy*,
September 2004.

Patent Infringements

Brad Stone, "Google's Page: Apple's Android Pique 'For Show,'" *Bloomberg Businessweek*, April 4, 2012. http://www.businessweek.com/articles/2012-04-04 /googles-page-apples-android-pique-for-show.

Closed Systems

Larry Page, Q & A at Zeitgeist Americas 2012 (video). https://www.youtube.com/watch?v=4Mzlp6mIaC4.

Open vs. Closed Systems

Steven Levy, "Google's Larry Page on Why Moon Shots Matter," *Wired*, January 17, 2013. http://www.wired .com/business/2013/01/ff-qa-larry-page/.

Open-Source OS Driving Innovation

Larry Page, "2012 Update from the CEO," Google Investor Relations. http://investor.google.com /corporate/2012/ceo-letter.html.

Facebook's Major Fail

Matt Peckham, "Axis of Suppression: China, Facebook and Iran, Says Google's Sergey Brin," *Time*, April 16, 2012. http://techland.time.com/2012/04/16 /axis-of-suppression-china-facebook-and-iran-says -googles-sergey-brin/.

Facebook's Closed Data

Interview with Larry Page, *Charlie Rose*, PBS, May 21, 2012.

Microsoft Contemplates Buying Yahoo

Jordan Robertson, "Google's Brin: Microsoft Bid 'Unnerving,'" Associated Press, February 21, 2008.

Microsoft's Search-and-Destroy Strategy

Adi Ignatius, "In Search of the Real Google," *Time*, February 20, 2006. http://content.time.com/time /magazine/article/0,9171,1158961,00.html.

Opportunities Untapped

Steven Levy, "Google's Larry Page on Why Moon Shots Matter," *Wired*, January 17, 2013. http://www.wired .com/business/2013/01/ff-qa-larry-page/.

Staying Focused

"The Lost Google Tapes," Sergey Brin and Larry Page interview with John F. Ince, January 2000, quoted in John F. Ince, "The Lost Tapes: Conversations Tape-Recorded in the Early Years With Google's Founders Illuminate How Their Actions Forged the Growth of a Silicon Valley Giant," *San Francisco Chronicle*, December 3, 2006. http://www.sfgate.com/opinion/article /THE-LOST-TAPES-Conversations-tape -recorded-in-2544534.php#photo-2640696.

Web Portals

David Sheff, "Playboy Interview: Google Guys," *Playboy*, September 2004.

Forward Thinking

Larry Page, "Google Q1 2013 Earnings Call," Google IR (video), April 18, 2013. http://www.youtube.com /watch?v=JGI2TMQGdJ4&feature=c4-overview&list =UU9RZRAPdKRM91k1XwbELJEg.

Leverage

Ken Auletta, *Googled: The End of the World as We Know It*, 2009. New York: Penguin Books. Kindle edition.

Mobile

Evelyn M. Rusli, "Google's Big Bet on the Mobile Future," *New York Times*, August 15, 2011. http://dealbook .nytimes.com/2011/08/15 /googles-big-bet-on-the-mobile-future/?_r=0.

Mobile Devices Monetized

Larry Page, Q & A at Zeitgeist Americas 2012 (video). https://www.youtube.com/watch?v=4Mzlp6mIaC4.

Business Principles

Commercialization

Steven Levy, "Google's Larry Page on Why Moon Shots Matter," *Wired*, January 17, 2013. http://www.wired .com/business/2013/01/ff-qa-larry-page/.

Product Line Focus

Larry Page, "2012 Update from the CEO," Google Investor Relations. http://investor.google.com/corporate/2012 /ceo-letter.html.

Dual Voting Class Stock Structure

Google, Amendment 9 to Form S-1, filed August 18, 2004. http://www.sec.gov/Archives/edgar /data/1288776/000119312504142742/ds1a.htm.

"It's best to do one thing really, really well."

"Ten Things We Know to Be True," Google company website. www.google.com/about/company/philosophy.

Hiring Smart People

Adam Lashinsky, "100 Best Companies to Work For: Can Google Three-peat?," *Fortune*, January 31, 2008. http://money.cnn.com/2008/01/28/news

/companies/google.qa.fortune/index
.htm?postversion=2008012908.

Hiring Passionate People

Adam Lashinsky, "100 Best Companies to Work For: Can
Google Three-peat?," *Fortune*, January 31, 2008. http://
money.cnn.com/2008/01/28/news/companies/google
.qa.fortune/index.htm?postversion=2008012908.

Money

Adi Ignatius, "In Search of the Real Google," *Time*,
February 20, 2006.
http://content.time.com/time
/magazine/article/0,9171,1158961,00.html.

Strategy

Adi Ignatius, "In Search of the Real Google," *Time*,
February 20, 2006. http://content.time.com/time
/magazine/article/0,9171,1158961,00.html.

Auction-based IPO

Google, Amendment 9 to Form S-1, filed August 18,
2004. http://www.sec.gov/Archives/edgar
/data/1288776/000119312504142742/ds1a.htm.

Trust in Results

Adam Lashinsky, "100 Best Companies to Work For: Can
Google Three-peat?," *Fortune*, January 31, 2008.
http://money.cnn.com/2008/01/28/news
/companies/google.qa.fortune/index
.htm?postversion=2008012908.

Media and Advertising

Media

Larry Page, address at the American Association for the
Advancement of Science, San Francisco, February
2007. http://www.abc.net.au/radionational
/programs/scienceshow/changing-the-world
---larry-page/3394966#transcript.

Advertising (in 1999)

Karsten Lemm, "Hier Völlig in Ordnung," *Stern*
magazine, January 1999. http://www.ubergizmo
.com/2008/09/googles-first-steps/.

Advertising Campaigns

John F. Ince, "The Lost Google Tapes Part 3" (podcast),
January 2000. http://www.podtech.net/home/1758
/podventurezone-lost-google-tapes-part-3-sergey-brin.

AdWords

Google, Annual Report, 2006. http://investor.google.com
/pdf/2006_google_annual_report.pdf.

Ethics of Advertising

David Sheff, "Playboy Interview: Google Guys," *Playboy*,
September 2004.

Paid Inclusion Ads

David Sheff, "Playboy Interview: Google Guys," *Playboy*,
September 2004.

Winning

Douglas Edwards, *I'm Feeling Lucky: The Confessions
of Google Employee Number 59*, 2011. New York:
Houghton Mifflin Harcourt. 47.

"You can make money without doing evil."

"Ten Things We Know to Be True," Google company
website. www.google.com/about/company/philosophy.

User Experience

Tardiness

Karsten Lemm, "Hier Völlig in Ordnung," *Stern*
magazine, January 1999. http://www.ubergizmo
.com/2008/09/googles-first-steps/.

Service as a Goal

Google, Amendment 9 to Form S-1, filed August 18, 2004.
http://www.sec.gov/Archives/edgar
/data/1288776/000119312504142742/ds1a.htm.

"Fast is better than slow."

"Ten Things We Know to Be True," Google company
website. www.google.com/about/company/philosophy.

"Focus on the user and all else will follow."

"Ten Things We Know to Be True," Google company
website. www.google.com/about/company/philosophy.

Seamless Product Integration

Larry Page, "2012 Update from the CEO," Google Investor
Relations. http://investor.google.com/corporate/2012
/ceo-letter.html.

Simplicity

Mickey Butts, Interview with Larry Page for FT Dynamo,
August 6, 2001. http://mickeybutts.com/google.html.

User Is Never Wrong

Sergey Brin interview for *.com–LIVE* by Leslie Walker, *Washington Post*, November 4, 1999. http://www.washingtonpost.com/wp-srv/liveonline /business/walker/walker110499.htm.

Personal Information

Greg Jarboe, "A 'Fireside Chat' with Google's Sergey Brin," *Search Engine Watch*, October 15, 2003. http://searchenginewatch.com/article/2064259 /A-Fireside-Chat-with-Googles-Sergey-Brin.

Computer Cookies

Ken Auletta, "Annals of Communications: The Search Party," *New Yorker*, January 14, 2008. http://www.newyorker.com /reporting/2008/01/14/080114fa_fact_auletta.

Company Culture

Scaling

Mickey Butts, Interview with Larry Page for FT Dynamo, August 6, 2001. http://mickeybutts.com/google.html.

Reorganizing Company Divisions

Sergey Brin, speech at the Web 2.0 Summit, 2011, quoted in Brad Stone, "The Education of Google's Larry Page," *Bloomberg Businessweek*, April 4, 2012. http://www .businessweek.com/articles/2012-04-04 /the-education-of-googles-larry-page.

Dogs and Cats

Google, Code of Conduct, Google Investor Relations, http://investor.google.com/corporate /code-of-conduct.html.

Company Mantra

David Sheff, "Playboy Interview: Google Guys," *Playboy*,
    September 2004.

Startup Mindset

Larry Page, "2012 Update from the CEO," Google
    Investor Relations. http://investor.google.com
    /corporate/2012/ceo-letter.html.

Company as Family

Adam Lashinsky, "100 Best Companies to Work For:
    Larry Page: Google Should Be Like a Family," *Fortune*,
    January 19, 2012. http://tech.fortune.cnn
    .com/2012/01/19/best-companies-google-larry-page/.

Health Care

Adam Lashinsky, "100 Best Companies to Work For:
    Larry Page: Google Should Be Like a Family," *Fortune*,
    January 19, 2012. http://tech.fortune.cnn
    .com/2012/01/19/best-companies-google-larry-page/.

Core Areas

Harry McCracken and Lev Grossman, "The Audacity of
    Google: Larry Page and the Art of the Moon Shot,"
    Time, September 30, 2013.

Corporate Culture Is Dynamic

Adam Lashinsky, "100 Best Companies to Work For: Can
    Google Three-peat?," *Fortune*, January 31, 2008.
    http://money.cnn.com/2008/01/28/news
    /companies/google.qa.fortune/index
    .htm?postversion=2008012908.

Open Communications

"Our Culture," Google company website. http://www
.google.com/about/company/facts/culture.

Job Titles

Douglas Edwards, *I'm Feeling Lucky: The Confessions
of Google Employee Number 59*, 2011. New York:
Houghton Mifflin Harcourt. 13.

"You can be serious without a suit."

"Ten Things We Know to Be True," Google company
website. www.google.com/about/company/philosophy.

20 Percent Solution

Google, Amendment 9 to Form S-1, filed August 18, 2004.
http://www.sec.gov/Archives/edgar
/data/1288776/000119312504142742/ds1a.htm.

Timidity

Ken Auletta, "Annals of Communications: The Search
Party," *New Yorker*, January 14, 2008. http://www
.newyorker.com/reporting/2008/01/14
/080114fa_fact_auletta.

Leadership

Seeking a CEO

John F. Ince, "The Lost Google Tapes Part 4" (podcast),
January 2000. http://www.podtech.net/home/1771
/podventurezone-lost-google-tapes-part-4-sergey-brin.

Larry's Rules of Order

Douglas Edwards, *I'm Feeling Lucky: The Confessions
of Google Employee Number 59*, 2011. New York:
Houghton Mifflin Harcourt. 123.

L-Team

Brad Stone, "The Education of Google's Larry Page,"
    Bloomberg Businessweek, April 4, 2012.
    http://www.businessweek.com/articles/2012-04-04
    /the-education-of-googles-larry-page.

The Job of a Leader

Adam Lashinsky, "100 Best Companies to Work For:
    Larry Page: Google Should Be Like a Family," *Fortune*,
    January 19, 2012. http://tech.fortune.cnn
    .com/2012/01/19/best-companies-google-larry-page/.

Dual CEOs

Mickey Butts, Interview with Larry Page for FT
    Dynamo, August 6, 2001. http://mickeybutts.com
    /google.html.

Organizational Challenges

"The Lost Google Tapes," Sergey Brin and Larry Page
    interview with John F. Ince, January 2000, quoted in
    John F. Ince, "The Lost Tapes: Conversations Tape-
    Recorded in the Early Years With Google's Founders
    Illuminate How Their Actions Forged the Growth
    of a Silicon Valley Giant," *San Francisco Chronicle*,
    December 3, 2006. http://www.sfgate.com/opinion/
    article
    /THE-LOST-TAPES-Conversations-tape
    -recorded-in-2544534.php#photo-2640696.

Youthful CEO

Sergey Brin and Larry Page interview for Academy of
    Achievement, London, October 28, 2000. http://www
    .achievement.org/autodoc/page/pagoint-1.

"Adult Supervision"

Interview with Sergey Brin, *Charlie Rose*, PBS, July 2001, quoted in Scott Austin, "About Eric Schmidt's 'Adult Supervision' Comment," *Wall Street Journal Venture Capital Dispatch* (blog), January 20, 2011. http://blogs.wsj.com/venturecapital/2011/01/20/about-eric-schmidts-adult-supervision-comment/.

Success and Failure

Ambition

Larry Page, "Beyond Today," speech at Zeitgeist 2012 (video). https://www.youtube.com/watch?v=YoWH-CoFwn4.

Ambition and Failure

Steven Levy, *In the Plex: How Google Thinks, Works, and Shapes Our Lives*, 2011. New York: Simon and Schuster. 12.

Challenges

Larry Page, University of Michigan commencement speech, May 2, 2009. http://googlepress.blogspot.com/2009/05/larry-pages-university-of-michigan.html.

Changing the World

Larry Page, University of Michigan commencement speech, May 2, 2009. http://googlepress.blogspot.com/2009/05/larry-pages-university-of-michigan.html.

Crazy Ones in Business

Andy Serwer, "Larry Page on How to Change the World," *Fortune*, May 1, 2008. http://money.cnn.com/2008/04/29/magazines/fortune/larry_page_change_the_world.fortune/index.htm.

Internal Risk

Andy Serwer, "Larry Page on How to Change the World,"
Fortune, May 1, 2008. http://money.cnn
.com/2008/04/29/magazines/fortune
/larry_page_change_the_world.fortune/index.htm.

Fear of Failure

Andy Serwer, "Larry Page on How to Change the World,"
Fortune, May 1, 2008. http://money.cnn
.com/2008/04/29/magazines/fortune
/larry_page_change_the_world.fortune/index.htm.

Mega-Ambitious Goals

Larry Page, "2012 Update from the CEO," Google
Investor Relations. http://investor.google.com
/corporate/2012/ceo-letter.html.

Other Ventures

Optimistic Future

Andy Serwer, "Larry Page on How to Change the World,"
Fortune, May 1, 2008. http://money.cnn
.com/2008/04/29/magazines/fortune
/larry_page_change_the_world.fortune/index.htm.

Philanthropy

Mark Malseed, "The Story of Sergey Brin," *Moment*,
February–March 2007. http://www.momentmag.com
/the-story-of-sergey-brin/.

Hybrid Philanthropy

Larry Page, "Towards More Renewable Energy," Google
Official Blog, November 27, 2007. http://googleblog
.blogspot.com/2007/11
/towards-more-renewable-energy.html.

Space Tourism

Space Adventures, "Google Co-Founder Sergey Brin
    Announced as Space Adventures' Orbital Spaceflight
    Investor and Founding Member of Orbital Mission
    Explorers Circle" (press release), June 11, 2008.
    http://www.spaceadventures.com/index
    .cfm?fuseaction=news.viewnews&newsid=615.

Aiming High

Harry McCracken and Lev Grossman, "The Audacity of
    Google: Larry Page and the Art of the Moon Shot,"
    Time, September 30, 2013.

$331,450 Hamburger

Sergey Brin, "Introducing Cultured Beef" (video),
    Maastricht University Cultured Beef/Department of
    Expansion. http://culturedbeef.net/.

Calico, Google's Health-Care Initiative

Larry Page, personal post on Google+, September 18,
    2013. https://plus.google.com/+LarryPage/posts
    /Lh8SKC6sED1.

Genetic Predisposition for Parkinson's Disease

Sergey Brin, "LRRK2," *Too* (personal blog), September 18,
    2008. http://too.blogspot.com/2008/09/lrrk2.html.

Mars—or Bust!

Google, "Larry Page and Sergey Brin on Virgle" (video),
    http://www.google.com/virgle/pioneer.html.

Life Lessons

Dreams

Larry Page, University of Michigan commencement
speech, May 2, 2009. http://googlepress.blogspot
.com/2009/05/larry-pages-university-of-michigan.html.

Family as Priority

Larry Page, University of Michigan commencement
speech, May 2, 2009. http://googlepress.blogspot
.com/2009/05/larry-pages-university-of-michigan.html.

Feynman, Theoretical Physicist

Sergey Brin and Larry Page interview for Academy of
Achievement, London, October 28, 2000. http://www
.achievement.org/autodoc/page/pagoint-1.

Frugality

Mark Malseed, "The Story of Sergey Brin," *Moment*,
February–March 2007. http://www.momentmag.com
/the-story-of-sergey-brin/.

Great Expectations

Sergey Brin, speech to Israeli students, September 2003,
quoted in Mark Malseed, "The Story of Sergey Brin,"
Moment, February–March 2007. http://www
.momentmag.com/the-story-of-sergey-brin/.

Goal Setting

Larry Page, speech to Israeli students, September 2003,
quoted in David A. Vise and Mark Malseed, *The
Google Story: Inside the Hottest Business, Media and
Technology Success of Our Time, Updated Edition for
Google's 10th Birthday*, 2008. New York: Bantam Dell.
Kindle edition.

Growing Up in the United States, and Not Russia

Sergey Brin and Larry Page interview for Academy of Achievement, London, October 28, 2000. http://www.achievement.org/autodoc/page/pagoint-1.

Meetings

Larry Page, address at the American Association for the Advancement of Science, San Francisco, February 2007. http://www.abc.net.au/radionational/programs/scienceshow/changing-the-world---larry-page/3394966#transcript.

Steve Jobs

Larry Page, personal post on Google+, October 5, 2011. https://plus.google.com/+LarryPage/posts/4wkYwTCCgAc.

Striking Employees

Adam Lashinsky, "100 Best Companies to Work For: Google Wins Again," *Fortune*, January 29, 2008. http://money.cnn.com/2008/01/18/news/companies/google.fortune/index.htm.

Wealth

Adi Ignatius, "In Search of the Real Google," *Time*, February 20, 2006. http://content.time.com/time/magazine/article/0,9171,1158961,00.html.

Working 24/7

Sergey Brin and Larry Page interview for Academy of Achievement, London, October 28, 2000. http://www.achievement.org/autodoc/page/pagoint-1.

Standing Up for Your Principles

Stephanie Sammartino McPherson, *Sergey Brin and Larry Page: Founders of Google,* USA Today Lifeline Biographies, 2010. Minneapolis: Twenty-First Century Books. 82.

Excerpts from 2004 Founders' Letter

Google, Amendment 9 to Form S-1, filed August 18, 2004. http://www.sec.gov/Archives/edgar /data/1288776/000119312504142742/ds1a.htm.

Milestones

2001

"A press release dated August 6....": Google, "Google Names Dr. Eric Schmidt Chief Executive Officer" (press release), August 6, 2001. http://googlepress .blogspot.com/2001/08/google-names-dr-eric-schmidt-chief.html.

"2001 interview on *Charlie Rose*, in which Rose asked...": Sergey Brin, Interview with Charlie Rose, *Charlie Rose*, PBS, July 2001, quoted in Scott Austin, "About Eric Schmidt's 'Adult Supervision' Comment," *Wall Street Journal Venture Capital Dispatch* (blog), January 20, 2011. http://blogs.wsj.com/venturecapital/2011/01/20 /about-eric-schmidts-adult-supervision-comment/.

2004

"Urs Hölzle points out in an official Google blog entry...": Urs Hölzle, "They Might Be Giants, or Just Standing on Them," Google Official Blog, October 22, 2004.

http://googleblog.blogspot.com/2004/10
/they-might-be-giants-or-just-standing.html.

2007

"Apple CEO Tim Cook, in *Bloomberg Businessweek*,
September 19, 2013, disparages...": Sam Grobart,
"Apple Chiefs Discuss Strategy, Market Share—
and the New iPhones," *Bloomberg Businessweek*,
September 19, 2013. http://www.businessweek.com
/articles/2013-09-19/cook-ive-and-federighi-on-the
-new-iphone-and-apples-once-and-future-strategy.

2008

"In a Google blog entry dated September 23, Google's
Erick Tseng...": Erick Tseng, "The First Android-
Powered Phone," Google Official Blog, September 23,
2008. http://googleblog.blogspot.com/2008/09
/first-android-powered-phone.html.

2012

"As a Google spokesperson told *The Verge*...": Amar
Toor, "New Google Glass UI Video Shows Off Search,
Camera, and Voice Translation Features," *The Verge*,
February 20, 2013. http://www.theverge
.com/2013/2/20/4008180
/google-glass-ui-previewed-in-new-video.

"But like I said....": Miguel Helft, "Fortune Exclusive:
Larry Page on Google," *Fortune*, December 11, 2012.
http://tech.fortune.cnn.com/2012/12/11/larry-page/.

ABOUT THE EDITOR

George Beahm has published more than 30 books, including *I, Steve: Steve Jobs In His Own Words* (Agate B2, 2011), *The Boy Billionaire: Mark Zuckerberg In His Own Words* (Agate B2, 2012), and a book on media mogul Rupert Murdoch.

Beahm is a former Army major, a Field Artillery Officer who held a top-secret clearance. He served on active duty with the First Infantry Division (Fort Riley, Kansas); he subsequently served in the Virginia Army National Guard and in the Army Reserve.

He lives with his wife, Mary, in southeast Virginia.